...as expressed by

Stephanie Salvatore, Nashville, Tennessee

*Send us **your** expression of **"Life.*** *For more information e-mail darin.clark@lifeway.com*

Creative Group

STEVE GLADEN
General Editor

JAY STROTHER, BRIAN GASS, AND BRIAN DANIEL
Writers

BRIAN DANIEL
Editorial Project Leader

BRIAN GASS
Content Editor

DARIN CLARK
Art Director & Designer

JESSICA WEAVER
Production Editor

PHIL DAVIS
Marketing

LOUANN DICKSON, LYNNE WEAVER, AND NATHAN SLEDGE
Production

RICK HOWERTON AND RON KECK
Small Group Life Consultants

TABLE OF CONTENTS

EPISODE 1, SCENES 1-6

FROM THE EDGE OF LIFE

Like so many people, I have tended to compartmentalize my spiritual pilgrimage. There are some parts allocated to different areas of life while other parts are relegated to certain seasons of life. But these words by Richard Foster struck a chord with me: "We are always being formed spiritually." As I took this statement to prayer, I thought back to my days as the oldest son of a single parent; to a college experience lacking direction; to the discipline of my time in the Navy; to the earliest days of marriage and family. In each place, God revealed to me how He has shaped me through experiences—more than a few I would have wished to be spared from, quite frankly. During these times I have been formed, transformed, and reformed. I have also been able to identify those moments when the Villain was successful in his efforts to deform.

This first episode of *Small Group Life* has been created to take you on a journey into your own spiritual formation. As you and the group engage these Scenes, be on alert for what God has to say to you about the journey He has called you into. These are the deep matters of the heart. These are the moments that make a lifetime. This is God's curriculum of life.

Brian C. Daniel

Brian Daniel
Editorial Project Leader, *Small Group Life*

HOW TO USE SMALL GROUP LIFE

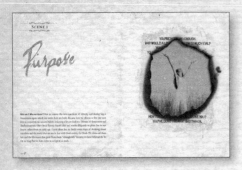

Scene Introduction

An introductory paragraph has been included to prime the group for your small-group conversation. Also, the graphic opposite the introductory paragraph(s) is no accident. We recommend asking group members to interact with these images in devotional settings outside of group time.

Connect

It's unreasonable to assume your group can go "zero to sixty" without some intermediate step. Connect includes an icebreaker and a relevant quote. The quote can be incorporated into the group discussion or used as a mid-week (or off-week) "teaser" for the next *Small Group Life* meeting.

Quote

Grow

Grow is the heart of the *Small Group Life* experience. This is the Bible study portion of your small-group time. Grow employs an incremental discipleship model. *Small Group Life* has been created to guide groups on a redemptive journey that leads to incremental discipleship and spiritual growth—building healthy disciples along the way. It has been streamlined to help your group remain engaged, manage time, and stay on task. Look for callout material that provides additional background or insights pertinent to your conversation.

Callout

Second Take

The Second Take is a second look at any given topic. It has been included as an additional small-group experience for groups wishing to spend more time in any of the topics or for groups who meet weekly.

Serve/Go

Serve/Go develops ministry and leadership through missional challenges. The Serve/Go can be done by the entire group together, or an individual may choose to do it alone.

Scripture Notes and Commentary

Commentary notes are associated with the Scriptures featured during Grow. Scripture notes:

- provide additional depth
- add biblical background and context
- contribute unique insights

Small(er) Group Life

Small(er) Group Life summarizes how the children interacted with the Scene's theme during their time together. This page provides:

- follow-up questions that reinforce biblical learning and spiritual growth and provide an entrance into spiritual conversation with your children
- easy-to-lead family devotions

Video Downloads

Videos are available online to enhance your *Small Group Life* experience. Our video downloads are designed to be shown either during group sessions or watched by group members before getting together. Videos can be downloaded at *www.lifeway.com/smallgrouplife*.

Leader Notes and Leader's Guide

Small Group Life includes Leader Notes to help the group facilitator create the best small-group environment. These notes have several functions:

- contribute to leader development
- provide additional instruction
- add insight to specific questions

A Leader's Guide starts on page 104 and provides specific instructions on materials needed and the flow of the meeting for the group leader.

STUDY THEME

Episode 1

spiritual formation

Spiritual formation is perhaps best defined as the process of being conformed into the image of Christ for the sake of others. It is broad enough to include the ways the Accuser, our enemy, works to deform us; the ways God works to reform us; and the transformation that emerges as a result of God's redemptive work.

Because we are spiritual beings, created for an eternity, we are always in the process of being formed spiritually. Every thought we hold, every decision we make, every action we take, every emotion we allow to shape our behavior, every response we make to the world around us, every relationship we enter into, every reaction we have toward the things that surround us—each contributes to our formation. Very often our spiritual formation can be ascribed to the hidden work of God.

In this Episode of *Small Group Life,* you're going to be looking at your formation as it relates to six different areas: purpose, the Enemy, redemption, atonement, mystery, and community. Not only are these the foundations of our spiritual lives but they are also the areas where we are formed. As you engage these experiences, prayerfully consider the formative moments you've experienced along the way and how God continues to be at work in your life and in the lives of the members of your small group.

While you're discussing these topics related to Formation, your children can also be exploring the same issues in a broader sense. We've added Small(er) Group Life so that kids can be learning spiritual formation instead of simply being baby-sat during your time together. Lesson plans for Small(er) Group Life are on the web at *www.lifeway.com/smallgrouplife,* and a page at the end of each Scene will help you to review with your kids what they've learned. I think you'll love this new twist to "building" into your kids.

Steve

Steve Gladen , Saddleback Church
General Editor

Notes:

Purpose

Who am I? Why am I here? How we answer the twin questions of identity and destiny lays a foundation upon which our entire lives are built. Because how we choose to live our seen lives is rooted in our unseen beliefs, believing a lie can lead to a lifetime of frustration and disillusionment. Our Great Enemy knows this and works diligently to plant lies in our hearts, often from an early age. Upon these lies we build entire ways of thinking about ourselves and the world that are not in line with God's reality, the Truth. We often call these lies and the life issues that grow from them "strongholds," because we have believed the lie for so long that we have come to accept it as truth.

YOU'RE NOT GOOD ENOUGH.
WHY WOULD A LOV........LOW SO MUCH EVIL?
YOU AR.....
YOU ARE.....

YO.......AN.YONE.
HOW COUL.....PER.ON LIKE YOU?
YOU'VE DONE TOO MANY BAD THINGS.

CONNECT

10 min.

1. **Take turns as you introduce yourselves and answer the question: When you were a kid, what did you want to be when you "grew up," and why?**

2. **Our motivation can reveal a lot about our understanding of how God created us uniquely. If you were going to climb a mountain, which of the explanations below is closest to the reason you would give? Explain.**

- ○ It looks like fun.
- ○ I love a good challenge.
- ○ I want to see the view from the top.
- ○ I want to prove to myself that I can do it.
- ○ It's easier than tunneling through the mountain.
- ○ It's in my way.
- ○ Because it's there.

"Don't ask what the world needs. Ask what makes you come alive, and go do it. Because what the world needs is people who have come alive."

—Howard Thurman

3 What activities, interests, or hobbies make you feel most alive in life?

GROW

40–50 min.

Leader: Read this paragraph aloud to the group.

Most of us are painfully oblivious to the ways that God is forming us through the many experiences—good and bad—that life offers and to the purposes our spiritual formation can serve. Today we're going to use the story of Gideon, a man who didn't feel like he was enough, to frame our group discussion.

At the point our story begins, Israel has had 40 years of peace. Sadly, they once again chose to do evil in God's eyes, so He allowed the Midianites to oppress them. The Israelites became a people in hiding, barely surviving. The cycle continued for generations and became culturally ingrained. Then God decided to intervene ...

Leader: You may wish to share with your group more background to this passage from the notes on page 22.

11 **The Angel of the LORD came ... Gideon was threshing wheat in the wine vat in order to hide it from the Midianites.** 12 **Then the Angel of the LORD appeared to him and said: "The LORD is with you, mighty warrior."**
13 **Gideon said to Him, "Please Sir, if the LORD is with us, why has all this happened? And where are all His wonders that our fathers told us about? ... The LORD has abandoned us and handed us over to Midian."** JUDGES 6:11-13

Leader/Question #1: Provide time for members to relate to Gideon and share from their own stories.

1. READ JUDGES 6:11-13. ABANDONED. THAT'S A TOUGH CHARGE AGAINST GOD. WHAT EMOTIONS DO YOU THINK GIDEON WAS STRUGGLING WITH AS A RESULT OF THIS BELIEF? HAVE YOU FELT THAT WAY BEFORE?

Leader/Question #2: Challenge group members to avoid pat or rote answers.

2. WHAT DO YOU THINK GOD SAW IN GIDEON? WHY GIDEON? WHY NOW?

Leader: Point to the information below. How important is God's revelation for us today?

"Angel of the LORD"

How God chooses to reveal Himself is up to His sovereign choice alone. We should remember that in the epoch of history we live in, we have God's revelation in the Bible. Previous generations have not always had the benefit of written revelation. Gideon needed revelation of a different type. God can and does speak in many ways; however, all revelation should be validated through a scriptural lens.

3. DESCRIBE GIDEON'S RESPONSE TO THE ANGEL OF THE LORD. WHAT DO YOU THINK THIS SUGGESTS ABOUT GIDEON'S CONCLUSIONS ABOUT GOD AND THE WORLD AROUND HIM?

4. WHAT ARE THE IMPLICATIONS OF HIS CONCLUSIONS?

The LORD turned to him and said "Go in the strength you have and deliver Israel from the power of Midian. Am I not sending you?"
JUDGES 6:14

5. WHAT DO YOU THINK THE LORD MEANT BY THE "STRENGTH" THAT GIDEON POSSESSED?

Leader / Question #6: Too often we focus on hiding our weaknesses instead of acknowledging that we are God's image-bearers.

6. THE ENEMY'S STRONGHOLDS ARE DISRUPTED AS WE RESPOND TO GOD'S CALL BY LIVING OUT OF OUR STRENGTHS. LIST SOME OF THE UNIQUE STRENGTHS THAT YOU THINK GOD HAS GIVEN YOU.

Leader: Spiritual reformation begins at the point of accepting God's authority in your life.

"Please do not leave this place until I return to You. Let me bring my gift and set it before You."
And He said, "I will stay until you return." JUDGES 6:18

7. WHAT DO YOU THINK ABOUT GIDEON'S RESPONSE? WHAT DOES IT SHOW ABOUT HIS HEART?

Leader / Question #8: Encourage authenticity within the group discussion by responding first.

8. GIDEON WAS WILLING TO CONFRONT HIS SENSE OF POWERLESSNESS. WHAT IS THE UNIQUE PART OF YOUR STORY OR BACKGROUND THAT YOU THINK GOD IS WAITING FOR YOU TO BRING AND SET BEFORE HIM?

Gideon did indeed go in the strength he had and was able to deliver Israel from the power of Midian. As you become aware of how God wants to use your own story, you will begin to fulfill your own unique purpose.

Leader: Close in prayer or transition to Serve/Go, found on page 21.

2nd Take

CONNECT

10 min.

Leader: Depending on time, choose one question, or answer both. Go around the group on question 1 and let everyone share. Then go around again on question 2.

1 **Which of the following did you have the hardest time waiting for when you were growing up?**

- ○ Christmas
- ○ Summer vacation
- ○ When I would be able to drive
- ○ When I could move out of the house
- ○ My birthday
- ○ Puberty
- ○ When I would turn 18
- ○ Other _____

2 **Which of the following do you have the hardest time waiting for now?**

- ○ The next episode of my favorite TV show
- ○ Christmas
- ○ Payday
- ○ The weekend
- ○ My vacation
- ○ Other _____

GROW

So much of our language and culture has addressed one of the epic topics: the meaning of life. Purpose and meaning seem elusive for so many. Purpose is a noble and worthwhile pursuit, but one that has often been frustrating to understand. God uses our own stories and experiences to reveal His purpose for our lives.

Leader/Question #1: Ask the group to consider the process of discovering their purpose.

1. WHEN IT COMES TO YOUR PURPOSE, DOES IT SOMETIMES SEEM LIKE YOU'VE BEEN WAITING FOR A LONG TIME FOR AN "AHA" MOMENT? WHY OR WHY NOT?

> **"I know the plans I have for you," declares the LORD, "plans to prosper you and not to harm you, plans to give you hope and a future."** JEREMIAH 29:11, NIV

2. READ JEREMIAH 29:11. GOD HAS A SPECIFIC PLAN FOR YOUR LIFE. HOW DOES THAT MAKE YOU THINK DIFFERENTLY ABOUT YOUR FORMATION AND PURPOSE?

12 You will call to Me and come and pray to Me, and I will listen to you. 13 You will seek Me and find Me when you search for Me with all your heart. JEREMIAH 29:12-13

Leader/Question #3: Challenge group members to consider what the truth about their purpose requires of them.

3. READ JEREMIAH 29:13. HOW DO YOU THINK YOU'RE SUPPOSED TO DRAW FROM ALL OF YOUR HEART IN ORDER TO STEP INTO THE ROLE YOU HAVE BEEN CREATED TO PLAY? WHAT DOES IT TAKE TO CONNECT YOUR HEART TO GOD'S?

Let's turn our attention back to the story of Gideon and his unique circumstances. Gideon has responded to God and gathered an army to take on the Midianites. God has given him specific instructions and now the battle awaits.

Leader/Question #4: Challenge the group to consider Gideon's journey as they think through their own spiritual pilgrimage.

4. DESCRIBE HOW YOU THINK GIDEON MAY HAVE SEARCHED HIS OWN HEART TO FIND THE STRENGTH HE NEEDED TO BE THE PERSON HE WAS CREATED TO BE.

The three companies blew their trumpets and shattered their pitchers. They held their torches in their left hands, their trumpets in their right hands, and shouted, "The sword of the Lord and of Gideon!" JUDGES 7:20

Leader/Questions #5 & #6: Ask members to pay close attention to what the companies in 7:20 shouted.

5. READ JUDGES 7:20. HOW DO YOU THINK THIS CLIMACTIC SHOUT VALIDATED GIDEON AND THE ROLE HE PLAYED IN GOD'S PLAN? WHAT UNCOMFORTABLE CIRCUMSTANCES, LIES, OR CORE BELIEFS DID HE HAVE TO CONFRONT TO GET TO THIS POINT?

6. WHAT LIES DO YOU THINK YOU HAVE EMBRACED THAT MIGHT BE STANDING BETWEEN YOU AND THE ROLE GOD HAS CALLED YOU TO PLAY IN THIS WORLD?

Gideon and his army followed God and rid the land of the Midianites forever.

22 Then the Israelites said to Gideon, "Rule over us, you as well as your sons and your grandsons, for you delivered us from the power of Midian."
23 But Gideon said to them, "I will not rule over you, and my son will not rule over you; the LORD will rule over you." JUDGES 8:22-23

Leader/Questions #7 & #8: Note how confident Gideon is as a leader and in his relationship with God.

7. WHAT TEMPTATIONS DID GIDEON FACE AFTER FINDING HIS PURPOSE? HOW HAD HE CHANGED AS A PERSON?

8. HOW WOULD YOU LIKE TO SEE YOUR OWN STORY DEVELOP SIMILARLY? WHAT IS STOPPING THIS FROM HAPPENING?

Discovering and putting purpose into practice is oftentimes a life's work. With all the forces at play and the unpredictable nature of the world around us, it takes both intention and patience to realize a measure of spiritual formation. Most of all, it requires a heart that continually cries out to God.

Leader: Close in prayer or transition to Serve/Go, found on page 21.

SERVE ☞ GO

10 min.

Here is an opportunity to contribute missionally to your community. There are five other opportunities—one for each Scene—if you choose not to participate this week.

Just as Gideon was willing to give from his resources, we have opportunities to make a Kingdom impact with ours. Low-income single parents are especially vulnerable to food and housing hardship because their wages must cover all of their family's costs—a difficult feat with one paycheck. Almost half of single parents report food and housing hardships. Remember, these are only suggestions.

> **In the next week, identify a single parent who ...**
> › Needs their oil changed
> › Wants to send their children to a camp
> › Has special maintenance needs
> › Faces a specific financial challenge
> › Needs a second person to get a child to a certain destination
>
> **... and commit your group to serve them.**

Scripture Notes

Judges 6:11-13 The oppression of the Midianites forced Gideon to do his threshing in a nearly impossible way: in a partially enclosed winepress. Gideon's present state did not show him at all to be a "mighty warrior," as the angel of the LORD called him. Instead of responding in awe, Gideon complained about why God would allow evil against His chosen people (ignoring the role Israel played in bringing judgment on herself).

Judges 6:14 Gideon's strength was to be found in the Lord; Gideon's strength on his own was in no way adequate for the task presented to him.

Judges 6:18 Gideon wanted evidence of a miracle before he would commit to action.

Judges 7:20 Regularly, only leaders would blow the ram's horn. Three hundred horns would signify to the Midianites a huge attack force immediately upon them.

Jeremiah 29:12-13 These verses come in the midst of Yahweh's promise that He would fulfill His plan for Israel's future—after 70 years of Babylonian captivity.

Judges 8:22-23 The people's request of Gideon—and his ancestors—to rule over them was very flawed from a spiritual eye. It had nothing to do with God's deliverance, and it copied the Canaanite culture of dynastic rule. Gideon refused both the kingship and future dynastic rule.

Prayer

Name	Request / Praise	Answered

Scripture Notes are excerpted from the *Holman Old Testament Commentary* and *Holman New Testament Commentary* Series. Max Anders, general editor (Nashville: B&H Publishing Group, 1998–2009).

Howard Thurman quote is from "Howard Thurman Quotes," ThinkExist.com [online], 2006 [accessed 17 April 2009]. Available from the Internet: *www.thinkexist.com*.

Memory Verse

"For we are God's workmanship, created in Christ Jesus to do good works, which God prepared in advance for us to do."
Ephesians 2:10, NIV

SMALL GROUP Life

What they experienced

Through the Bible story about Gideon, the children learned that God created them with special likes, dislikes, talents and abilities—all to serve Him. They also learned that Jesus is a friend they can count on!

Scene 1: Family Devotion Idea

Your children were asked the question, "If you could take a day off from school and do anything you wanted, what would you do?" Ask your children how they answered that question.

Talk about how everyone is unique—influenced by friends, television, movies, books, and family.

2nd Take: Family Devotion Idea

Discuss with your children what you learned about purpose and how God has created each of us with specific purposes in mind.

Family activity

Make cookies together and take them to an elderly neighbor or church member. Serve God together.

As any good counselor will tell you, you've got to start by going back to the root of the issue and identify what went wrong and when, if you're going to have any hope of understanding the full impact of your life experiences. So for today's meeting we go back to that place in time when paradise was lost, so we can understand what we're up against. If we have any hope of being a transformed people, then we're going to have to understand how we've been deformed in the first place.

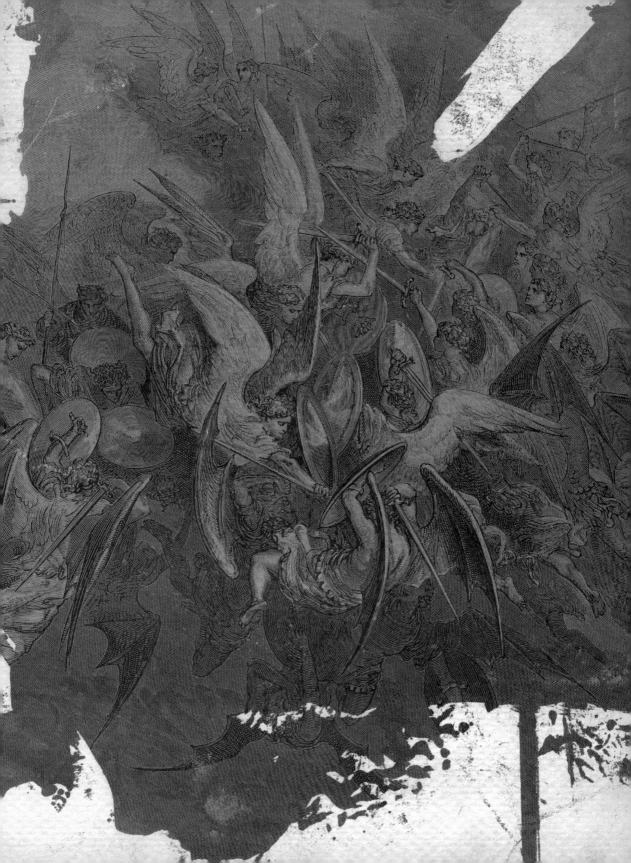

CONNECT

1 Imagine that as an adult you could choose to wield a single superpower. Which one would you choose?

- ○ Flight
- ○ X-Ray Vision
- ○ Invisibility
- ○ Time Travel
- ○ Super Speed
- ○ No actual super-power, but like Batman, almost unlimited resources to create cool crime-fighting gadgets
- ○ I already have a super-power. That power is _____.

2 Every superhero has a cause worth fighting for. What evil force in the world would you choose to combat with your superpower?

"Satan mounted his rebellion through the power of one idea: God doesn't have a good heart."

John Eldredge

GROW

40–50 min.

Leader: *Read this passage aloud to the group.*

Evil originated during a period best described as the "time before time." Long before Genesis 1 there was harmony between God and the created beings: the angels. One created being, Lucifer, was brightest among them all.

Leader: *Consider the pre-rebellion Satan—then known as Lucifer.*

[12] **Shining morning star, how you have fallen from the heavens! You destroyer of nations, you have been cut down to the ground.** [13] **You said to yourself: "I will ascend to the heavens; I will set up my throne above the stars of God. I will sit on the mount of the gods' assembly, in the remotest parts of the North.** [14] **I will ascend above the highest clouds; I will make myself like the Most High."** ISAIAH 14:12-14

[14] **"You were an anointed guardian cherub, for I had appointed you. You were on the holy mountain of God; you walked among the fiery stones. ...** [17] **Your heart became proud because of your beauty; For the sake of your splendor you corrupted your wisdom. So I threw you down to the earth; I made a spectacle of you before kings."** EZEKIEL 28:14,17

Leader/Question #1: Think about the motivation and the consequences of misuse as you consider these attributes.

1. Name some of the characteristics attributed to Lucifer in these passages from Isaiah and Ezekiel. What do you think corrupted Lucifer?

Leader/Question #2: Remember that this rebellion takes place before recorded events during a "time before time"—even before Genesis.

2. Ezekiel 28:17 reveals to us that this insurrectionist was thrown down to the earth. In what ways do you think this rebellion shows itself in our world today?

Larger Story

The story that has been in motion since eternity in both the "seen" and "unseen" realities, where we each have a part to play and the plot is bigger than we are, a reality where the stakes are much higher. Small stories, by contrast, are limited to our individual lives, birth to death, in the seen world where the main plot is about us—you—and you are the central character.

3. HOW DO YOU THINK THIS "GREATER REALITY" OR LARGER STORY MIGHT AFFECT THE WAYS WE ARE FORMED SPIRITUALLY?

Pride swelled within Lucifer who, with a third of the angels, led an insurrection against God, was ultimately defeated, and was cast into our domain where he has diminished (but still potent) power. He is forced to rely upon scheming, cunning, and deception. While banished, this fallen one is driven to deform, abuse, and distort our spiritual formation—luring us away from what is truest about us as God's image-bearers.

It's important to remember, though, that although Satan and a third of the angels fell, God was and is in control. Two-thirds of the angels stayed obedient and work with God on our behalf. Still, the Enemy found his way into the garden of Eden.

---

4 "No! You will not die," the serpent said to the woman. 5 "In fact, God knows that when you eat it your eyes will be opened and you will be like God, knowing good and evil." 6 Then the woman saw that the tree was good for food and delightful to look at, and that it was desirable for obtaining wisdom. So she took some of its fruit and ate it; she also gave some to her husband, who was with her, and he ate it. GENESIS 3:4-6

4. WHAT DO YOU THINK GENESIS 3:4-6 REVEALS ABOUT THE TACTICS AND SCHEMES OF THE ENEMY, OUR ADVERSARY? WHAT WEAKNESSES DID THE ENEMY CHOOSE TO EXPLOIT IN ADAM AND EVE?

5. CONSIDER THE OPENING THE ENEMY FOUND IN ADAM AND EVE. HOW DO YOU THINK WE CAN IDENTIFY AREAS IN OUR OWN LIVES THAT COULD BE EXPLOITED BY THE ENEMY?

Finally brothers, whatever is true, whatever is honorable, whatever is just, whatever is pure, whatever is lovely, whatever is commendable—if there is any moral excellence and if there is any praise—dwell on these things. PHILIPPIANS 4:8

6. READ PHILIPPIANS 4:8. DISCUSS SOME PRACTICAL WAYS THAT WE CAN PROTECT OURSELVES FROM THE TACTICS AND SCHEMES OF THE ENEMY.

Leader: Close in prayer or transition to Serve/Go, found on page 37.

SCENE 2

2nd Take

CONNECT

15 min.

Leader:

Cue the *Gladiator* DVD to the beginning of **chapter 6**, "You Will Not Be Emperor."
Start at the beginning of the scene (**31:48**) and play through **36:01**.

Like every great story, ours also has a Villain. Though limited in power, the Enemy has been given sway over this world. He is a deceiver who seeks to destroy. Today's Connect begins with a scene about a villain. Watch this 4-minute clip from the movie *Gladiator* and answer the questions that follow.

1 Discuss the "virtues" Commodus gives to his father as reasons to support his own claims to power. Do you think these virtues are inherently bad? If so, why? If not, why not choose Commodus instead of General Maximus?

2 Given what you know, how does the villain of *Gladiator* compare to the way the Villain in the Larger Story is described in Isaiah 14 and Ezekiel 28? (See pp. 28-29.)

GROW

40–50 min.

The Enemy is not alone in his great endeavor to deform us. Though limited in number and finite in power, Satan and his minions roam the earth looking for any weakness to exploit. According to Scripture, they are tireless.

Leader: Choose to read the verses below, or ask for volunteers.

And no wonder! For Satan himself is disguised as an angel of light. 2 CORINTHIANS 11:14

Leader/Question #1 & #2: Encourage the group to consider the implications of their conclusions.

1. READ 2 CORINTHIANS 11:14 AND THINK AGAIN ABOUT COMMODUS IN THE CLIP FROM *GLADIATOR*. WHAT DO YOU THINK THIS SAYS ABOUT TRUSTING THE APPEARANCE OF THINGS? DISCUSS A TIME WHEN YOU WERE DECEIVED BY APPEARANCES.

[7] He cried out with a loud voice, "What do You have to do with me, Jesus, Son of the Most High God? I beg You before God, don't torment me!" [8] For He had told him, "Come out of the man, you unclean spirit!"
[9] "What is your name?" He asked him. "My name is Legion," he answered Him, "because we are many." MARK 5:7-9

2. THIS FRIGHTENING SCENE FROM MARK 5 REMINDS US THAT THE ENEMY'S HELPERS ARE MANY. WHAT ARE SOME LESS OBVIOUS WAYS PERHAPS, YET NO LESS THREATENING, THAT YOU HAVE SEEN THE ENEMY'S FORCES AT WORK IN THE WORLD AROUND YOU?

Be sober! Be on the alert! Your adversary the Devil is prowling around like a roaring lion, looking for anyone he can devour.
1 PETER 5:8

"A thief comes only to steal and to kill and to destroy ..."
JOHN 10:10A

Leader/Question #3: Ask the group to be specific.

3. WHAT IS THE GOAL OF THE DEVIL, THE THIEF, AS DESCRIBED IN 1 PETER 5 AND JOHN 10? WHAT DO YOU THINK IS LITERALLY AT STAKE IN YOUR LIFE?

Leader/Question #4: This question ultimately asks about the real Villain in the story—is it only our fallen nature or is there more?

4. IN AN EARLIER MEETING WE TALKED A LITTLE ABOUT OUR WEAKNESSES, HOW TO IDENTIFY THEM, AND HOW TO PROTECT OURSELVES FROM THE ENEMY'S TACTICS AND SCHEMES. WHERE DO YOU THINK OUR WEAKNESSES COME FROM? ARE WE BORN WITH THEM OR DO YOU THINK THEY EMERGE AS A RESPONSE TO SOME EVENT OR CIRCUMSTANCE?

We know that our old self was crucified with Him in order that sin's dominion over the body may be abolished, so that we may no longer be enslaved to sin. ROMANS 6:6

Surely you desire truth in the inner parts; you teach me wisdom in the inmost place. PSALM 51:6, NIV

Leader/Question #5: Remind members that, statistically, Christians are not very different from nonbelievers where issues like addictions and divorce rates are concerned.

5. ROMANS 6:6 SAYS THAT SIN NO LONGER HAS CONTROL OVER THE LIFE OF A BELIEVER. SO WHY DO YOU THINK WE MIGHT CONTINUE TO LIVE IN WAYS THAT ARE LESS-THAN-FREE?

Leader/Question #6: We are formed most by what we REALLY believe, not by what we say we believe.

6. READ PSALM 51:6 ABOVE. IT REFERS TO TRUTH IN "THE INNER PARTS." IN SOME TRANSLATIONS IT IS TRUTH IN THE "INMOST BEING." WHAT DO YOU THINK IS THE DIFFERENCE BETWEEN THIS TRUTH IN THE CORE OF WHO WE ARE VERSUS THE THINGS WE SAY OR THINK WE BELIEVE?

"… I have come that they may have life and have it in abundance." JOHN 10:10B

¹ **The Spirit of the Lord God is on Me,**
because the Lord has anointed Me
to bring good news to the poor.
He has sent Me to heal the brokenhearted,
to proclaim liberty to the captives,
and freedom to the prisoners;
² **to proclaim the year of the Lord's favor,**
and the day of our God's vengeance;
to comfort all who mourn,
³ **to provide for those who mourn in Zion;**
to give them a crown of beauty instead of ashes,
festive oil instead of mourning,
and splendid clothes instead of despair. ISAIAH 61:1-3A

Leader/Question #7: This question asks us to consider how Jesus wants to spiritually reform us.

7. JESUS READ FROM ISAIAH 61 WHEN HE ANNOUNCED HIMSELF IN LUKE 4. HOW DO YOU THINK JESUS PLANS TO "UNDO" THE WORK OF THE ENEMY IN YOUR LIFE? IN WHAT WAYS HAVE YOU SEEN HIM WORK TO DEMOLISH THE STRONGHOLDS OF THE ENEMY ALREADY?

8. IN WHAT WAYS DO YOU NEED JESUS TO HEAL BROKEN HEARTS IN YOUR LIFE, FAMILY, CHURCH, OR COMMUNITY TODAY?

The origin of evil is only part of the story. The biggest part is, of course, the way the Enemy continues to distort our perceptions and tirelessly probe for our weaknesses—weaknesses that emerge from our own fallen nature. Combating the Enemy on our own is impossible. Our only hope is the healing grace of Jesus—who has proclaimed to set free the captives and bind up our broken hearts.

Leader: Close in prayer or transition to Serve/Go, found on page 37.

SERVE ☞ GO

— 10 min.

God doesn't rescue us from the Enemy just for our own good; He also uses our transformed hearts as part of His plan to help others. There is an enormous amount of pain and guilt in our world. In today's church we often insulate ourselves to this pain by spending the vast majority of our time in the Christian subculture of our church and community. Spend some time brainstorming ways that you can place yourself "next" to others who are experiencing brokenness in their lives right now. Choose one of those people to reach out to this week.

> **Here are a few ideas to get you started, but once you open your eyes to the needs around you, you won't have to look far:**
>
> › The Bible says "love your neighbor as yourself," but many of us don't even know our neighbors very well. In your neighborhood there is likely someone who lives alone. Invite them to join you for one meal this week and get to know their story.
>
> › Our society is stressful on marriages, especially for those with children. Offer a free night of baby-sitting to a two-career couple with young children and you might help save a marriage.
>
> › With the rise of e-mail and social network applications, writing notes or cards of encouragement has become a lost art. The good news is that it makes receiving a hand-written note that much more meaningful. Is there a coworker or family member you have encountered who could use some building up right now?
>
> **Come prepared to share with the group next week the story of the person you reached out to. But for now, go around the group and write the names below of the persons each one in your group thinks is their person to minister to. Compare results next week.**
>
> › _____   › _____
>
> › _____   › _____
>
> › _____   › _____

SCRIPTURE NOTES

Isaiah 14: 12-14 Most High. The Hebrew word Elyon, an ancient poetic name for God. May be an ancient name used in Jerusalem before Israel conquered the city, and then used by Israel to express the universal rule of God. **morning star.** The planet Venus, understood by Israel's neighbors as a god. Literally, this passage is about the fall of the proud Babylonian king who wanted divine authority.

Ezekiel 28:14,17 This passage is a lament against the king of Tyre. Because he was deluded by his own accomplishments, he would be rejected by God and thrown to the earth. Because of his successful trade practice, he had become haughty (one of the things God hates, Proverbs 6:16-17).

Genesis 3:4-6 The very first doctrine that Satan denied in Scripture was to insinuate God's word was not always true. In verse 5, he questions the goodness of God as well. Satan implied God's welfare was at man's expense. Eve fulfilled her God-given desires in a sinful manner. While Eve's sin followed the pattern laid out in 1 John 2:16, the difference is that Eve did not have a sinful nature. **gave some to her husband who was with her, and he ate it.** Sinners have a way of involving others and validating one another with their sin. (See Romans 1:32.)

Philippians 4:8 true. Anxiety comes when false ideas and unreal circumstances occupy the mind instead of truth. **honorable.** Lofty, majestic, awesome; above the world's dirt and scandal. **just.** Fair to all parties involved; fulfills all obligations and debts. **pure.** Encompasses all of life; concentrating on pure thoughts leads one away from sin and toward God and worship. **lovely.** A rare word referring to things that attract, please, and win other people's admiration and affection. **commendable.** Worthy of praise or approval.

Mark 5:7-9 We see a wrestling match occur in the possessed man's soul. The demon may or may not have known the implications of the title *Son of the Most High God*. In the first century, many believed to know someone's name was in a sense to control him. Jesus perhaps asks the demon's name for the benefit of the crowd around Him. **Legion.** A legion consisted of 6,000 soldiers. This may not have been the number of demons in this man, but it was clear a whole army of demons possessed him.

John 10:10 The Good Shepherd provides for His sheep, unlike thieves who steal, kill, and destroy. By purchasing the "sheep" with His blood (v. 11), He provides them with "life in abundance."

Romans 6:6 Believers have been "crucified with Him" so we can have the benefits the dead enjoy—freedom from sin.

Isaiah 61:1-3 The time when God would display His "favor" was indefinite, but it would come. And, of course, it came through the Messiah, who used this passage to declare His role in Luke 4. Through Christ, God would comfort, crown, and bring gladness to the one who once mourned.

PRAYER

Name	Request / Praise	Answered

Scripture Notes are excerpted from the *Holman Old Testament Commentary* and *Holman New Testament Commentary* Series. Max Anders, general editor (Nashville: B&H Publishing Group, 1998–2009).

John Eldredge quote is taken from Brent Curtis and John Eldredge, *The Sacred Romance: Drawing Closer to the Heart of God* (Nashville: Thomas Nelson, 1997), 76.

Memory Verse

"Be self-controlled and alert. Your enemy the devil prowls around like a roaring lion looking for someone to devour."
1 Peter 5:8, NIV

Small G̶r̶o̶u̶p̶ er Life

What they experienced

The children learned that evil does exist. It is not just in fairy tales and movies. Situations and people are not always what they first appear to be. The children also learned the importance of telling the whole truth—nothing less, nothing more.

Scene 1: Family Devotion Idea

Your children learned about how there is a consequence for sin. Are you consistent with giving consequences to your children for inappropriate or appropriate behavior? The next time you need to give a "consequence" to them, make sure you explain that choice equals consequence. Let your children pick an appropriate punishment. You might be surprised by what they choose!

2nd Take: Family Devotion Idea

Your children were given examples of "embellishing" the truth. How many times have you "stretched the truth"? Does this ring a bell: "I've told you a MILLION times to clean up your room"? Your children will imitate your behavior.

Family activity

Have a conversation with your children about "embellishing" the truth. Ask them to help you. Ask them to let you know when they hear you "stretching the truth." Be ready—you're going to get caught!

SCENE 3

In the journey of formation, we have to come to grips with the reality that life gets messy. In the middle of that mess, we may believe that we aren't good for much of anything anymore, much less for what God is doing. What we forget is that the Larger Story that surrounds us is much less about us and more about God. In this session we'll explore how God invites us as full participants in the process of reshaping us to understand how God "buys back" the messy parts of our lives. God doesn't miss or forget a thing we've gone through, and He wants to use our total experience to shape us for His purposes. We call this mysterious but hope-filled part of our rescue story the drama of redemption.

CONNECT

10 min.

1 If Hollywood were to film a drama based on your life, what actor or actress would you want to play you, and why?

2 The idea of "redemption" is a central theme of many movies. If you were the central character of one such movie, what popular movie title would best describe your life right now? Explain.

- ○ *Braveheart*
- ○ *The Illusionist*
- ○ *Signs*
- ○ *Awakening*
- ○ *Parenthood*
- ○ Create-Your-Own: _____

God isn't quite done with you yet. So, my friend — shall we see if He still offers redemption?

Mohinder Suresh, "Heroes"

3 **Has there ever been a time in your life when you wanted a new start more than anything else? Describe that experience.**

GROW

40–50 min.

Leader: Read this paragraph aloud to the group.

We've heard the word used over and over again but it remains a mystery to most: *redemption*. We have become so used to living in a broken world that we're more familiar and comfortable with other words: loss, pain, and anger, to name a few. So we're a bit stunned to discover that it's not only us who are longing for a change but the entire world as well.

"All have sinned and fall short of the glory of God."
ROMANS 3:23

"The creation eagerly waits with anticipation for God's sons to be revealed." ROMANS 8:19

Leader/Question #1: Remind the group to think more toward the Larger Story implications.

1. READ ROMANS 3:23. WHAT IS YOUR UNDERSTANDING OF "ALL" AND "FALL SHORT" HERE? WHAT ARE SOME WAYS THAT YOU HAVE FALLEN SHORT IN LIFE THAT CAUSE YOU TO NEED REDEMPTION?

Leader/Question #2: Follow up with thoughts about the implications of total redemption.

2. WHAT DO YOU THINK ROMANS 8:19 SAYS ABOUT THE TOTALITY OF NOT ONLY THE FALL OF HUMANITY BUT ALSO THE TOTALITY OF REDEMPTION? HOW MIGHT OUR REDEMPTION AFFECT THE WHOLE CREATION?

We know that all things work together for the good of those who love God: those who are called according to His purpose.
ROMANS 8:28

Theodicy

Theodicy describes the ways that God interacts with us: prevention, intervention, redemption. We don't know how much suffering God actually protects us from, only that it is something less than 100 percent.

Leader/Question #3: Acknowledging God's supreme power, He still makes room for free will and for the Enemy to have a certain amount of liberty ... for now.

3. WHAT DO YOU THINK ROMANS 8:28 REVEALS ABOUT WHAT GOD CAUSES—SPECIFICALLY? WHAT DOES GOD NOT CAUSE?

4. SOME PEOPLE MAY FEEL THIS WAY: "MY PROBLEMS ARE TOO BIG (OR SMALL) FOR GOD" OR "GOD MIGHT LOVE ME, BUT I SURE DON'T BELIEVE THAT HE LIKES ME." CAN YOU RELATE? EXPLAIN.

Leader/Question #5: We often struggle with the tension between both the big and the personal nature of God.

5. HOW IS GOD'S PLAN FOR REDEMPTION BOTH LARGE AND SMALL ENOUGH TO DEAL WITH THE PROBLEMS WE CREATE FOR OURSELVES OR IN WHICH WE FIND OURSELVES TRAPPED?

I will repay you for the years that the swarming locust ate, the young locust, the destroying locust, and the devouring locust.
JOEL 2:25

Leader/Question #6: You might also consider the "Why?" inherent here. Why has God allowed these locusts?

6. THERE ARE ALL SORTS OF "LOCUSTS" IN OUR WORLD AND IN OUR LIVES THAT DO DAMAGE BOTH IN THE SHORT TERM AND LONG TERM. THESE ARE THE PROBLEMS, MESSES, AND DESTRUCTIVE PARTS OF OUR STORIES THAT WE INVITE OR GOD ALLOWS. LIST SOME OF THEM, BOTH BIG AND SMALL.

"Even the Son of Man did not come to be served, but to serve, and to give His life—a ransom for many." MARK 10:45

Leader/Question 7: Our Christlikeness is predicated on many circumstances. One of these is a willingness to participate in God's redemptive story.

7. JESUS WAS WELL AWARE OF HIS ROLE IN THE REDEMPTION PROCESS: MAKING HIMSELF A WILLING VESSEL THROUGH WHOM GOD IS ABLE TO BUY US BACK. WHAT DO YOU THINK IS OUR ROLE IN JESUS' REDEMPTIVE MISSION?

Leader: Close in prayer or transition to Serve/Go, found on page 53.

SCENE 3

2nd take

CONNECT

15 min.

Leader:

Begin by showing a clip from the movie *Heart and Souls*.
Cue the DVD to **1:14:00** and show through **1:19:48**. Then discuss the following questions.

In this film, four passengers of an ill-fated bus trip died at the same time that Robert Downey Jr.'s character, Thomas, was born. The characters are inseparably connected from then on, with a need for each of the "angels" to find redemption before they can go to heaven. In this clip, Thomas is able to help Charles Grodin's character, Harrison, complete his task on earth.

1 Harrison says, "I'm not even alive and I'm perspiring" just before he sings. In what ways besides the obvious was Harrison not alive? What kind of occurrences, beliefs, or lies do you think had brought him to this place of paralysis during his life?

2 Thomas confronts Harrison and says, "You died a failure because you were never willing to take a chance in life." How do you think Harrison's redemption leads to a change in attitude and understanding of who he is?

GROW

We "redeem" coupons for a certain amount off of a product. We "redeem" tickets in exchange for a prize. We're tempted to think that we earn these things: by cutting out the coupon, we worked for that savings. Redemption is similar: it is a dimension of our salvation in which God chooses to exchange our messy past for a hopeful future, or our poor choices for lessons learned that shape us into who He wants us to be.

Leader/Question #1: This question invites members to consider their role in the Larger Story we referred to earlier (p. 29).

1. HOW DO YOU THINK WE ARE CALLED TO PLAY A ROLE IN GOD'S ULTIMATE PLANS FOR REDEMPTION? ARE YOU AWARE OF A SPECIFIC ROLE THAT YOU COULD BE CALLED INTO RIGHT NOW?

Leader/Question #2: Encourage members to be specific.

2. GIVE SOME WAYS THAT GOD HAS SURPRISED YOU IN THE MIDDLE OF LIFE'S MESSES. HOW HAS THIS HELPED TO EQUIP YOU FOR YOUR ROLE IN THE REDEMPTION STORY?

---

¹⁹ The created world itself can hardly wait for what's coming next. ²⁰ Everything in creation is being more or less held back. God reins it in ²¹ until both creation and all the creatures are ready and can be released at the same moment into the glorious times ahead. Meanwhile, the joyful anticipation deepens.
ROMANS 8:19-21, THE MESSAGE

Leader/Question #3: Reference Romans 8:21. Be imaginative. Avoid settling for simple answers. What will the world look like, people, natural wonders, plants and animals ...?

3. WHAT DOES GOD'S REDEMPTION LOOK LIKE? WHAT DO YOU THINK THE SCENE WILL LOOK LIKE WHEN ALL IS "RELEASED" OR "SET FREE" AS THE BOOK OF ROMANS REVEALS?

"Their Redeemer is strong; the LORD of Hosts is His name. He will fervently plead their case so that He might bring rest to the earth." JEREMIAH 50:34

Leader/Question 4: Challenge the group to consider what is REALLY at stake.

4. IN OUR WORLD IT'S NOT A MILITARY BATTLE THAT WE FIGHT, BUT A SPIRITUAL ONE. WHY DO YOU THINK THIS IDEA OF A "STRONG REDEEMER" IS IMPORTANT TO US IN THE BATTLE FOR THE FORMATION OF OUR HEARTS?

14 Since the children are made of flesh and blood, it's logical that the Savior took on flesh and blood in order to rescue them by his death. By embracing death, taking it into himself, he destroyed the Devil's hold on death **15** and freed all who cower through life, scared to death of death.   HEBREWS 2:14-15, THE MESSAGE

Leader/Question #5: Describe His mission for you personally and encourage the group to do the same.

5. DESCRIBE JESUS AS THE HERO-REDEEMER IN OUR LIFE STORIES. DESCRIBE HIS MISSION IN REDEEMING YOU AND WHAT IT HAS MEANT TO YOU.

Leader/Questions #6: Talk about our fears and where they come from.

6. WHY DO YOU THINK SO MANY PEOPLE LIVE AS IF REDEMPTION ISN'T AN OPTION? WHAT DO YOU THINK STANDS BETWEEN US AND THE REDEMPTION GOD HAS FOR US?

Don't grieve God's Holy Spirit, who sealed you for the day of redemption. EPHESIANS 4:30

Leader/Question #7: Try to avoid the cliché theological response here. Instead, wrestle with the idea of confident hope in the midst of the mess.

7. THE WORD *SEALED* SEEMS PRETTY STRONG AS IT RELATES TO OUR REDEMPTION. HOW CONFIDENT ARE YOU THAT GOD'S REDEMPTION IS A CERTAINTY? HOW DOES THAT CHANGE YOUR OUTLOOK OF YOUR LIFE'S MESSINESS?

As the bridge of a popular worship song declares, "I'll never know how much it cost, to see my sins upon that cross." It's difficult for us to fathom what a great gift redemption truly is. The appropriate response can't even be summed up in words; our response is our lives. Will we live as the "free" people who we are and out of the overflow of a transformed heart? Or will we go on believing the lie that we're still prisoners and allow our hearts to be caged?

Leader: Close in prayer or transition to Serve/Go, found on page 53.

SERVE ☞ GO

10 min.

Mark Batterson, the pastor of National Community Church, has a core value that he constantly uses to challenge his church: "Love people most when they least expect it and when they least deserve it." It's a theme that is closely tied to redemption: in the middle of a situation in which we hit rock bottom, God meets us there with His love and grace.

One of the forgotten mission fields in nearly every community is the prison system. In 2008, the number of people incarcerated in the U.S. reached its highest level ever. More than 1 in 100 American adults are behind bars.

There are many ministries locally and nationally that have been effective in reaching out to prisoners with a powerful mix: a message of hope and practical help in the form of classes and workshops that prepare them for a better life when they get out.

> **Visit these Web sites to get a better idea of how these organizations are meeting the needs of prisoners.**

> › Prison Fellowship (*www.prisonfellowship.org*)
> › Angel Tree (*www.angeltree.org*)
> › PrisonNet Ministry Network (*www.prisonnet.org*)

GROUP IDEA

As a group, spend some time thinking about how you could be "agents of redemptive hope" in the lives of prisoners. Does anyone in your group know anyone personally who is behind bars who could use encouragement and maybe even a visit to remind them they aren't forgotten? Many churches partner with parachurch groups that have established ministries in prisons. Check with your pastor, discipleship pastor, or missions minister to see how your church is involved. When a parent goes to jail, it often leads to a tremendous strain on families and children. Is there some way your group can help a young mother in this situation or provide rides or birthday gifts for children?

SCRIPTURE NOTES

Romans 3:23 Moral failure is the cause for righteousness having to come from God. Jews and Gentiles have "all sinned" (aorist tense; a snapshot in time of the condition of the human race) and continue to "fall short" (present tense). When Paul said here "all have sinned," he used the same Greek words as he did in 5:12, when discussing the entrance of sin into the world through Adam. **fall short.** The image here is not one of absence, but of always being behind or late. Try as we might to live up to God's standard, we might as well be trying to catch a falling star.

Romans 8:19 The curse to which the Creator subjected His creation will finally be lifted when the coheirs inhabit the new heavens and new earth (Revelation 22:3). When the curse is lifted, the creation will once again be an Edenic environment suitable for the image-bearers of God to inhabit.

Romans 8:28 God called us to a holy life on the basis of His purpose and grace, and it is that purpose to which we have been called that this verse invites our submission. Our new life in the Spirit is based on God's good purposes for our lives, and that includes suffering. Read literally, it is easy to see why some consider this the greatest verse in Scripture. It tells us that nothing happens outside of God's plan for our good.

Jeremiah 50:34 Jeremiah contrasts Israel's helplessness with Yahweh's strength.

PRAYER

Name	Request / Praise	Answered

Scripture Notes are excerpted from the *Holman Old Testament Commentary* and *Holman New Testament Commentary* Series. Max Anders, general editor (Nashville: B&H Publishing Group, 1998–2009).

"Heroes" quote is from Season 2, Episode 2, "Lizards." Quote can be found at *http://www.imdb.com/title/tt1054841/quotes*.

Memory Verse

"And we know that in all things God works for the good of those who love him, who have been called according to His purpose."
Romans 8:28, NIV

SMALL GROUP L_{er}fe

What they experienced

The children learned the meaning of "ransom" and then heard about the ransom that was paid for their sin: the death of Jesus. Because Jesus paid the ransom, we have been set free.

Scene 1: Family Devotion Idea

Ask your children about the game they played called "Sin Gets Heavy." Ask them how they feel about what Jesus did for them.

2nd Take: Family Devotion Idea

Your children learned that when they meet Jesus, He will give them new names. Have you ever told your children why you picked the names you gave them? Perhaps the names had significant meaning to you. Share that with your children.

Family activity

Together, get a baby name book or use the Internet to look up the meaning of your children's names. Tell them what their names mean and how special they are to you, but that the new names they will receive will be even more special because they will come from Christ!

Atonement PAID IN

"These two things I know: I am a great sinner. And Christ is a great savior." John Newton, the converted slave-trader who became a pastor and penned the words to the song "Amazing Grace" spoke those words in the film about his life. Simple but profound, that statement drives to the heart of *atonement*—a word loaded with depth of meaning. Webster defines atonement as "reparation [payment] for an offense." As we "do life," we all make mistakes on our formative journeys. Our natural response is to allow those mistakes to overwhelm us with feelings of guilt and paralyze our spiritual progress. We feel there's nothing that we can do to make up for our struggles. Understanding atonement opens the door to deep and lasting change in our hearts, because it reveals the terrible and wonderful way that God chose to meet our great need: through the sacrifice of His own Son Jesus on the cross. Atonement serves as the doorway to the life we all want to live.

CONNECT

15 min.

Leader:

Begin by showing a clip from the movie *Stranger Than Fiction*. Show from the beginning of Scene 25 ("Unthinkable Error") at **1:34:43** to the end of the movie (**1:45:15**). If you are crunched for time, you can stop at 1:43:14, but you'll miss some of the resolution.

In this movie, we're invited to meet Harold Crick, an IRS accountant who leads a mundane existence until the day he begins to hear voices in his head. He soon discovers these "voices" are the words of critically-acclaimed author Karen Eiffel, and he is the subject of her latest work. The only problem: the book is about a man who is headed toward his demise. Realizing his life is a "tragedy," Harold decides to make the most of it. This scene is the climactic moment of the movie, as Harold chooses to embrace his destiny, with one unexpected twist.

1 When Harold's girlfriend asked why he saved the boy, he responded, "I didn't have a choice. I had to." What effect do you think Harold's life story had on his conclusions here?

2 How do you think the boy might have responded to Harold if he had known the back story behind Harold's tough choice? How do you think we tend to view Jesus' sacrifice for us most of the time?

"Only one act of pure love, unsullied by any taint of ulterior motive, has ever been performed in the history of the world; namely, the self-giving of God in Christ on the cross for undeserving sinners."

— John Stott

3 Who is the person or persons to whom you think you owe the most in your life right now?

Leader: Encourage your group to reflect and share about people who have sacrificed and made a difference in their lives, especially those who have made sacrifices for them that they cannot repay.

GROW

40–50 min.

Leader: Read this paragraph aloud to the group.

This lesson is about the power—breadth, depth, height, and width—of atonement. Atonement clears the way for your new heart, your regeneration and transformation. If you are to be who God purposed in His heart for you to be, atonement had to take place. Let's take a look at how God helps us understand this life-changing process.

> *Primarily in the Old Testament, atonement refers to the process God established whereby humans could make an offering to God to restore fellowship with God. Such offerings, including both live and dead animals, incense, and money, were required to remove the bad effects of human sin.*

"He is to lay his hand on the head of the burnt offering so it can be accepted on his behalf to make atonement for him."
LEVITICUS 1:4

Leader / Question #1: This question will help members realize what they really believe to be true of God.

1. IF YOU HAVEN'T ALREADY, READ THE CALLOUT IN THE BOX ABOVE. WHY DO YOU THINK GOD REQUIRED AN ANIMAL SACRIFICE TO FORGIVE SIN AND RESTORE RELATIONSHIP WITH HIM? HOW IS THIS DIFFERENT FROM GOD'S ORIGINAL PLAN?

**The Lord God made clothing out of skins for Adam and his wife,
and He clothed them.** Genesis 3:21

*Leader / Question #2: This question will help members
understand what they really believe.*

2. Read Genesis 3:21. What do you think this act reveals about God's heart for us?
   In what ways do you think it is significant that the first blood ever shed was for
   Adam and Eve's comfort?

Just as God provided for Adam and Eve in the garden, even after their fall, we see God intervene later
in the lives of Abraham and Isaac.

[2] **"Take your son," He said, "your only son Isaac, whom you
love, go to the land of Moriah, and offer him there as a burnt
offering on one of the mountains I will tell you about." ... [11] But the
Angel of the Lord called to him from heaven and said, "Abraham,
Abraham!" He replied, "Here I am." [12] Then He said, "Do not lay
a hand on the boy or do anything to him." ... [13] Abraham looked
up and saw a ram caught by its horns in the thicket. So Abraham
went and took the ram and offered it as a burnt offering in place
of his son.** Genesis 22:2,11-13

3. Why would God put Abraham and Isaac in this situation?
   Why do you think God provided a sacrifice for them?

Leader/ Question #4: This question invites you into the tension between God's perfect mercy and His perfect justice.

4. HOW MIGHT THIS EVENT HAVE AFFECTED ABRAHAM AND ISAAC'S RELATIONSHIPS WITH GOD? TAKING GENESIS 3:21 AND THIS OCCURRENCE INTO ACCOUNT, WHAT DO YOU THINK THIS REVEALS ABOUT BOTH THE NEED AND THE PROVISION FOR ATONEMENT?

At one point in the Old Testament, God sent snakes into the camp of the Israelites because their hearts were so hard. After getting their attention, He commanded Moses to craft a bronze snake so that people would again be reminded to look to God for hope and for healing.

> [14] "Just as Moses lifted up the snake in the wilderness, so the Son of Man must be lifted up, [15] so that everyone who believes in Him will have eternal life." John 3:14-15

Leader/ Question #5: This question will make members more aware of the wonderful and supernatural aspect of atonement.

5. IN JOHN 3:14, JESUS COMPARED HIMSELF TO THE SNAKE IN THE WILDERNESS THAT MAGICALLY TRANSFORMED PEOPLE'S LIVES. WHY DO YOU THINK AUTHOR C.S. LEWIS WOULD DESCRIBE ATONEMENT AS "DEEP MAGIC"?

¹⁶ **"For God loved the world in this way: He gave His One and Only Son, so that everyone who believes in Him will not perish but have eternal life. ¹⁷ For God did not send His Son into the world that He might judge the world, but that the world might be saved through Him."** JOHN 3:16-17

Leader/Questions #6, #7, and #8: These questions are asked to help group members not just learn about but live out atonement.

6. JOHN 3:16 SAYS THAT GOD SENT HIS SON SO THAT THE WORLD MIGHT BE SAVED THROUGH HIM. TO BE SAVED IS TO BE CONFIDENT IN ETERNAL LIFE AND HEAVEN. DO YOU THINK THERE IS MORE TO BEING SAVED THAN A FUTURE PLACE IN HEAVEN? WHY OR WHY NOT?

7. FROM WHAT DO YOU THINK YOU HAVE BEEN SAVED?

8. IN ATONEMENT JESUS WILLINGLY TOOK WHAT WE HAD AND FREELY GAVE WHAT HE HAS. WHAT EFFECT DO YOU THINK THIS HAS ON YOUR SPIRITUAL GROWTH AND FORMATION?

Leader: Close in prayer or transition to Serve/Go, found on page 69.

SCENE 4

2nd Take

CONNECT

15 min.

Leader: Begin the session by singing a worship song your group is familiar with—either with a guitar or piano or a capella.

1. Growing up, did you have a favorite hymn or chorus that you remember? If you did, share that with the group.

2. What are some of the worship songs we sing today that are the most powerful for you? What is it about that song that makes a spiritual connection for you?

GROW

40-50 min.

Last week, we looked at why atonement was necessary and how it continues to bring healing to our lives. Let's look at some further implications that atonement has for our spiritual formation.

- -

⁴ He Himself bore our sicknesses and He carried our pains ... ⁵ He was pierced because of our transgressions, crushed because of our iniquities; punishment for our peace was on Him, and we are healed by His wounds. ⁶ We all went astray like sheep; we all have turned to our own way; and the LORD has punished Him for the iniquity of us all. ISAIAH 53:4-6

Leader/ Question #1: This is a passage that can be personally applied, so ask your group to do so.

1. ISAIAH 53:5 SAYS ONE RESULT OF THE ATONEMENT IS THAT OUR WOUNDS ARE HEALED. WHAT KIND OF WOUNDS DO YOU THINK THAT COVERS AND TO WHAT EXTENT ARE WE HEALED?

Leader/ Question #2: Have the group look back at some of the responses to John 3:14-17 from last week (pp. 62-63).

2. HOW DOES THAT HEALING TAKE PLACE? HOW HAS THAT LOOKED IN YOUR OWN LIFE?

"I will give you a new heart and put a new spirit within you; I will remove your heart of stone and give you a heart of flesh."
 EZEKIEL 36:26

"heart of flesh"

While the term flesh *is often associated with human weakness, here it represents a heart that is pliable and teachable. Nothing in this passage mentions Israel's participation in the transformation; it is all the work of God and should be credited as such.*

Leader/ Question #3: Members should consider the implication of the old suddenly gone, replaced with the new.

3. READ EZEKIEL 36:26. WHAT DO YOU THINK THIS NEW HEART—A HEART OF FLESH AS OPPOSED TO STONE—MEANS FOR US?

"I will place My law within them and write it on their hearts. I will be their God, and they will be My people." JEREMIAH 31:33B

Leader/Question #4: This new heart comes with a set of instructions.

4. HOW DOES THIS NEW HEART RESPOND TO GOD'S LAW WRITTEN UPON IT? WHAT ADVANTAGES DO YOU THINK IT GIVES FOLLOWERS OF CHRIST?

> **Therefore if anyone is in Christ, there is a new creation; old things have passed away, and look, new things have come.**
> 2 CORINTHIANS 5:17

Leader/Question #5: This is a good opportunity to reflect on the changes that have taken place in members' lives.

5. WHAT ARE SOME OF THE OLD THINGS THAT HAVE PASSED FROM YOUR LIFE? WHAT ABOUT THE NEW THINGS THAT HAVE COME?

Leader/Questions #6 and #7: These questions seek to connect what happened historically to what can happen practically in our lives.

> **We all, with unveiled faces, are reflecting the glory of the Lord and are being transformed into the same image from glory to glory; this is from the Lord.** 2 CORINTHIANS 3:18

6. SOME VERSIONS OF THE BIBLE TRANSLATE "GLORY TO GLORY" AS "EVER-INCREASING." HOW DO YOU THINK JESUS' ATONEMENT MAKES IT POSSIBLE TO LIVE WITH EVER-INCREASING GLORY?

50 **Jesus cried out again with a loud voice, and yielded up His**
spirit. **51** **And behold, the veil of the temple was torn in two from**
top to bottom; and the earth shook and the rocks were split.
MATTHEW 27:50-51, NASB

7. BOTH MATTHEW 27:51 AND 2 CORINTHIANS 3:18 REFER TO A VEIL. WHAT DO YOU THINK HAS
   BEEN UNVEILED? WHAT NEEDS TO BE UNVEILED IN OUR LIVES FOR US TO LIVE AUTHENTICALLY
   BEFORE GOD AND OTHERS?

For followers of Christ who travel the journey of formation, atonement is not some vague theological construct: it is the gritty reality that God took our sin and our mess upon Himself in the sacrifice of Jesus on the cross. In *The Chronicles of Narnia*, C. S. Lewis allegorizes this terrible but wonderful truth as the "deep magic" that the forces of evil do not account for and cannot overcome. It should lead us all who live gratefully "under its spell" to a place of deep commitment.

Leader: Close in prayer using the exercise below or transition to Serve/Go, found on page 69.

Prayer Experience: Jesus Paid It All

As you conclude this session, come back to another great song of faith, "Jesus Paid It All." As you listen to the words of this song and/or reflect on the lyrics, write down on a blank piece of paper what you really need Jesus to "wipe clean" today. Allow what you write to move you into a time of prayer, recognizing that the atoning work of Jesus has "covered" your sin and guilt. Create a makeshift altar in the middle of the room at which you wad up, tear up, or destroy your piece of paper as a symbol of the sin and guilt you are releasing through Christ. If you are meeting in a home with a fireplace, you can even burn the papers carefully. Choose one person to voice a prayer to conclude your time together.

SERVE  GO

10 min.

One of the easily overlooked aspects of atonement is that Jesus had to humble Himself and come to our world as one of us in order to release mankind from the spell of sin. While He remained fully God, He became fully man as well. It's difficult to imagine the King of the Universe becoming like one of us! But that's exactly what He did, because the servant who rules is also the ruler who serves!

> **If Christ was willing to serve us, then we should humble ourselves and be willing to serve others. Challenge everyone in the group this week to find one way to serve others that doesn't call attention to themselves. No matter your job title or the number of degrees you have, look for chances to do things like …**
>
> › Visit an elderly neighbor or friend in the nursing home.
>
> › Serve a shift at the local homeless shelter or help pass out coats and blankets in the cold.
>
> › Volunteer at the area food or clothes pantry, helping them organize and sort donations.

SCRIPTURE NOTES

Genesis 3:21 Man's attempt to cover himself with leaves was appropriate but not adequate. God provided Adam and Eve clothing at the expense of the life of an animal. God expressed His grace in the face of sin and judgment.

Genesis 22:2,11-13 Human sacrifice, common in ancient paganism, was wrong for the righteous people belonging to the Lord; but here, God's command trumps cultural mores. **offered it as a burnt offering in place of his son**. When our timid faith becomes trusted faith, it can turn into triumphant faith. But it all begins with an acceptance of God's substitutionary atonement.

John 3:14-15 Moses lifted up the head of the snake. This Old Testament example displays how the cross provided a cure from the poison of sin, deliverance from the death of sin, and removal of the condemnation of sin. **lifted up.** Each time these words are used in John's gospel, they emphasize the centrality of the cross and the message of salvation (8:28; 12:32).

John 3:16-17 Nicodemus would have believed that God loved Israel, but not much in Jewish theology indicated that God loved the world. Verse 17 explains the "why" of verse 16.

Isaiah 53:4-6 He suffered because of our sins, so that we might be healed and find the life of peace. What's more, we went along our merry paths like dumb sheep, while God made the servant suffer with the load of sin and guilt that belonged to all of us.

2 Corinthians 5:17 Paul drew from Old Testament language here, drawing from the prophets who described a new world that God would create at the end of this age (Isaiah 66:22). "New creations" have begun the transformation that will prepare them for the new heaven and new earth.

Matthew 27:50 The King proved sovereign even over the time of His death. The loud cry was a shout of triumphal completion.

PRAYER

Name	Request / Praise	Answered

Scripture Notes are excerpted from the *Holman Old Testament Commentary* and *Holman New Testament Commentary* Series.
Max Anders, general editor (Nashville: B&H Publishing Group, 1998–2009).

Quote is from John Stott, *The Cross of Christ* (Downer's Grove, IL: InterVarsity Press, 1986), 212.

Memory Verse

"Therefore, there is now no condemnation for those who are in Christ Jesus."
Romans 8:1, NIV

SMALL GROUP Life

What they experienced

The children learned that God's love is unconditional. We cannot do anything to earn it or lose it.

Scene 1: Family Devotion Idea

The children did a craft project and made a handprint lamb. Ask your children why the lamb is so special. Put the lamb in a prominent place in your home to let them know you think the lamb is important.

2nd Take: Family Devotion Idea

The children learned that once they accept the love of God, their hearts are sealed and that love can never be taken away.

Family activity

The children were told that God's love is a gift. We do not have to earn it and we can never lose it. Get your children a special gift. A "just because I love you" gift. Wrap it and give the gift to them. It will be a nice surprise for your children, and it will give you an opportunity to reiterate your unconditional love and God's unconditional love.

Mystery

A quick glance at the Christian worldview often leads us to as many questions as answers: If God is good then why is there so much evil? How do I have real freedom, yet God is also in control of all things? And what about God Himself—three persons who are at the same time one being? It's enough to make smoke start coming out of your ears if you think about it for too long. At closer look, we discover that the Bible does have something to say about the mysteries of the faith and the human condition. But it's more like "signs pointing the way into a bright mist," as theologian N.T. Wright is fond of saying. If we believe that God is God and we are not, then we need to learn to live in the tension that we cannot know all things. We need to trust that God reveals to us enough at each stage of redemptive history so that we can know, trust, and follow His plan. As spiritual pilgrims on the journey of transformation, we need to learn to embrace mystery as one of the dynamic tensions of our faith.

CONNECT

Leader: Read the paragraph below to your group and ask them to share. In group life, it's often best to approach heavy subjects in a lighthearted way, so keep the conversation moving as you go.

Because he could not embrace the mysterious or the supernatural, Thomas Jefferson decided to rewrite the gospels without the parts he couldn't explain. Jefferson cut out every ~~miracle,~~ and the result was a book titled *The Life and Morals of Jesus of Nazareth* or what is commonly referred to as "the Jefferson Bible."

1. Jefferson had a difficult time coming to grips with the mysterious and miraculous. Which mysteries do you struggle with the most?

2. While we might not be as audacious as Jefferson, how do you think Christians sometimes approach God's revelation in much the same way?

I almost wish I hadn't gone down that rabbit hole — and yet — and yet — it's rather curious, you know, this sort of life! I do wonder what can have happened to me! When I used to read fairy tales, I fancied that kind of thing never happened, and now here I am in the middle of one!

Alice, from Alice in Wonderland

GROW

Leader: Read this passage aloud to the group.

Going back to Paul, the best Christian thinkers have always maintained that in the very real spiritual battle for our hearts, the known must be balanced by the unknown. God is a great mystery, unable to be boxed in by any of man's systems to explain Him, yet at the same time He makes Himself known to humanity in a myriad of ways. Let's consider some of God's mysteries.

> ⁶ **However, among the mature we do speak a wisdom, but not a wisdom of this age, or of the rulers of this age, who are coming to nothing. ⁷On the contrary, we speak God's hidden wisdom in a mystery, which God predestined before the ages for our glory.**
> 1 CORINTHIANS 2:6-7

Leader/Question #1 and #2: You might begin with a discussion of wisdom in general before exploring these two questions. For example, "How would you define wisdom?"

1. WHO ARE SOME PEOPLE WHOM YOU CONSIDER TO BE WISE? WHAT MAKES THEM SO?

2. GIVE SOME EXAMPLES OF THE "WISDOM OF THIS AGE." WHY DO YOU THINK THE WISDOM OF THIS AGE OR ITS RULERS MIGHT COME TO NOTHING, AS THIS PASSAGE TELLS US?

Leader/Question #3: Discuss God's relationship with mystery.

3. FIRST CORINTHIANS 2 REFERS TO GOD'S "HIDDEN WISDOM." WHY DO YOU THINK GOD MIGHT HIDE A PORTION OF HIS WISDOM FOR A TIME?

---

[8] **None of the rulers of this age knew it …** [9] **But as it is written: "What no eye has seen and no ear has heard, and what has never come into a man's heart, is what God has prepared for those who love Him."** 1 CORINTHIANS 2:8-9

Leader/Question #4: We should condition ourselves to pay particularly close attention when an idea is repeated for emphasis.

4. READ 1 CORINTHIANS 2:8-9: "NO EYE." "NO EAR." "NEVER COME INTO A MAN'S HEART." WHY DO YOU THINK THIS EXCLUSIVITY WOULD BE REPEATED AND EMPHASIZED? WHAT DO YOU THINK THIS SUGGESTS ABOUT WHAT LIES BEYOND OUR MIND'S CAPACITY TO IMAGINE?

Leader/Question #5: This question will encourage members to think beyond our physical limitations and senses.

5. HOW DO YOU THINK THAT WHICH WE DO NOT SEE STILL AFFECTS OUR SPIRITUAL FORMATION AND MOTIVATIONS? DISCUSS SOME OF THOSE UNSEEN, YET REAL, ASPECTS OF LIFE THAT CONTRIBUTE TO WHO WE ARE.

The Spirit searches everything, even the deep things of God.
1 CORINTHIANS 2:10

6. WHAT DO YOU THINK IS MEANT BY "DEEP THINGS OF GOD"? HOW DO YOU THINK THESE DEEP
   THINGS MIGHT CONTRIBUTE TO YOUR OWN SPIRITUAL FORMATION?

Consider Jacob's mysterious encounter with God in the Book of Genesis.

> [24] Jacob was left alone, and a man wrestled with him until
> daybreak. [25] When the man saw that He could not defeat him, He
> struck Jacob's hip as they wrestled and dislocated his hip socket.
> [26] Then He said to Jacob, "Let Me go, for it is daybreak."
> GENESIS 32:24-26

Leader/Question #7: This question should challenge us to consider how we feel about being completely honest with God.

7. LIKE JACOB, WE TOO ARE CALLED INTO THE MYSTERIOUS UNKOWN. GIVEN THIS ACCOUNT, IS
   THE UNKNOWN ALWAYS A SAFE PLACE TO BE? WHAT DOES JACOB'S EXPERIENCE TELL US ABOUT
   RISK-REWARD AND OUR OWN WILLINGNESS TO FACE AND WRESTLE WITH GOD?

²⁷ **"What is your name?" the man asked.**

"Jacob!" he replied.

²⁸ **"Your name will no longer be Jacob," He said. "It will be Israel because you have struggled with God and with men and have prevailed."**

²⁹ **Then Jacob asked Him, "Please tell me Your name."**

But He answered, "Why do you ask My name?" And He blessed him there.

³⁰ **Jacob then named the place Peniel, "For," he said, "I have seen God face to face, and I have been delivered." ³¹ The sun shone on him as he passed by Penuel—limping on his hip.**

GENESIS 32:27-31

Leader/Question #8: Again, we want members to consider how they feel about God's heart—who He is, what He enjoys, and so forth.

8. HOW DO YOU THINK GOD FELT ABOUT WRESTLING WITH JACOB?

There are two poles that tug at our hearts as we explore the dimensions of mystery. Our faith calls for living in this tension between the known and the unknown. Our spiritual formation is dependent on the awareness that there is great mystery surrounding our journey; there is always more going on than just what "meets the eye."

Leader: Close in prayer or transition to Serve/Go, found on page 85.

2ⁿᵈ Take

CONNECT

20 min.

Leader: Encourage group members to bring their Bibles, journals, and/or paper and be sure everyone has pens for this activity. Pray for 10 minutes as individuals and 10 minutes together.

We talk about the importance of spending time alone with God, but our hectic lives often get in the way. Today, we're going to experience an ancient discipline that helps us to meditate on Scripture. In silence, we can allow the Holy Spirit to speak to us. Move to different places around the room or perhaps to different locations. Meditate on Isaiah 42:16, a prayer of formation and restoration. Don't talk, and try to remain as quiet as possible. Use the following outline to shape your reflections:

› **Read.** Slow down and savor these words carefully. Read them over and over again, emphasizing certain words or phrases, allowing God to speak to you.

› **Think.** Ask the Holy Spirit to reveal to you the truth "hidden in plain sight" in these words. Consider how these ancient words speak to your current life story.

› **Pray.** Use these verses to shape a time of prayer. Write that prayer down.

› **Live.** Ask the Holy Spirit to guide you in how you are to act on what you just experienced.

Come back together and spend some time debriefing the experience:

› If you're comfortable doing so, share what the Holy Spirit revealed that was "hidden" to you before.

› Spiritual truth is sometimes a mystery to us, because we don't slow down long enough to hear the Spirit speak. What are practical ways we can build silence and spiritual reading into our lives?

GROW

The journey of our transformation takes on a new dimension when we begin to surrender our sense of self and choose to follow the voice of our mighty and mysterious God.

> **23 Just then a man with an unclean spirit was in their synagogue. He cried out, 24 "What do You have to do with us, Jesus—Nazarene? Have You come here to destroy us? I know who You are—the Holy One of God!" 25 But Jesus rebuked him and said, "Be quiet, and come out of him!" 26 And the unclean spirit convulsed him, shouted with a loud voice, and came out of him.** MARK 1:23-26

Leader/Questions #1 & #2: We don't often explore the dark side of mystery, but it's important for us to understand the battle for our hearts is not just a battle of "flesh and blood" (Ephesians 6:12).

1. THIS PASSAGE REVEALS SOME OF THE DARK REALITIES IN THE MYSTERIES OF THE SPIRITUAL WORLD. WHAT REAL SPIRITUAL DANGERS DO YOU THINK WE FACE IN THE PHYSICAL WORLD, IF ANY?

Demon Possession

The control of an individual's personality so that actions are influenced by an evil demonic spirit. Most of the New Testament references to demon possession appear in the Gospels and represent the outburst of satanic opposition to God's work in Christ. The cure for demonic possession was faith in the power of Christ. Never were magic or rituals used to deliver one from demonic possession.

2. WHAT DO YOU NOTICE ABOUT EVIL IN THE UNSEEN WORLD WHEN JESUS IS PRESENT? WHAT DO YOU THINK THIS SAYS ABOUT WHAT A DISCIPLE PROCLAIMING CHRIST MIGHT EXPECT?

Leader/Question #3: Lead with an example if possible.

3. IN WHAT WAYS, IF ANY, DO YOU SENSE THE ENEMY WORKING BEHIND THE VEIL OF THE SPIRITUAL WORLD, PERHAPS IN A WAY THAT AFFECTS YOU PERSONALLY?

[10] **Since He had healed many, all who had diseases were pressing toward Him to touch Him.** [11] **Whenever the unclean spirits saw Him, those possessed fell down before Him and cried out, "You are the Son of God!"** [12] **And He would strongly warn them not to make Him known.** MARK 3:10-12

Leader/Question #4: This question should help us understand better the tension between the seen and unseen worlds.

4. WHY DO YOU THINK JESUS WOULD WANT TO KEEP HIS IDENTITY A SECRET? WHAT DO YOU THINK THIS ENCOUNTER REVEALS ABOUT THE UNSEEN, SPIRITUAL WORLD BEHIND THE VEIL?

Just after this encounter with the unclean spirits, Jesus chose to mobilize His followers to better confront these evil forces.

> [13] Then He went up the mountain and summoned those He wanted, and they came to Him. [14] He also appointed 12—He also named them apostles—to be with Him, to send them out to preach, [15] and to have authority to drive out demons.   MARK 3:13-15

5. HOW DO YOU THINK JESUS' ENCOUNTER WITH THE DEMONS MIGHT HAVE FACTORED INTO HIS DECISION TO ORGANIZE HIS FOLLOWERS AT THIS TIME?

Leader/Question #6: Consider the motivational and inspirational role your small group plays in spiritual warfare.

6. IN THE DANGEROUS BATTLE FOR OUR HEARTS, WITH THE STAKES SO HIGH, HOW CAN WE FIND HOPE AND BE INSPIRED TO JOIN THE FIGHT?

Jesus later promised His followers that He would not leave them alone without wisdom in the dangerous battles they would face.

> [16] "I will ask the Father, and He will give you another Counselor to be with you forever. [17] He is the Spirit of truth. The world is unable to receive Him because it doesn't see Him or know Him. But you do know Him, because He remains with you and will be in you."
> JOHN 14:16-17

Leader/Question #7: Encourage the group to think about the different spiritual disciplines that can create an environment for listening and understanding.

7. READ JOHN 14:16-17. HOW DO YOU THINK YOU ARE SUPPOSED TO WORK WITH THE SPIRIT OF TRUTH TO DISCOVER THE HIDDEN WISDOM GOD HAS FOR YOU AND YOUR SPIRITUAL FORMATION? HOW DOES HE HELP YOU?

The journey of formation is not for the spiritually faint-at-heart, as we face a very real spiritual Enemy who seeks to destroy us. But while God can at times mystify us, He has also equipped us with a Counselor and Guide in the Holy Spirit, who searches the depths to convey to us truths about our lives, our stories, and our circumstances, things that cannot be discerned any other way.

Leader: Close in prayer or transition to Serve/Go found on page 85.

Serve  Go

10 min.

In the same way that wrestling with the mystery of God stretches our minds, participating in short-term missions stretches our faith. Mission experiences are places where we meet, up close and personal, the mystery of God.

> **The mysteries of life invite us into unfamiliar paths, and mission experiences provide opportunities to accept these invitations.**
> **Pray about the opportunities available to you to be more missional.**
>
> › At whose house could you have a party for neighbors, so that they can see Christ without anyone talking about Him?
>
> › Check with your church for information on contacting a state organization you can work with to do a day's ministering to your community.
>
> › Consider and pray about participating in a mission journey as a group. Have a home team who prays and an away team that goes. Not only are mission trips catalysts for encountering God and God's work in transforming new ways, but this experience will bring you closer than anything else you can do as a group.

Scripture Notes

1 Corinthians 2:6-7 wisdom of this age. Christian wisdom is the gospel, while the so-called wisdom of this age is the worldviews, sophistry, and belief systems which fail to recognize the gospel. **God's hidden wisdom.** The wisdom of Christ's crucifixion was first revealed when Christ came to minister on the earth, but it had been hidden in the secret counsels of God "before the ages."

1 Corinthians 2:8-9 While it might have seemed like earthly rulers such as Herod or Pilate understood God's wisdom because of their success on earth, their "wisdom" led them to crucify the Son of God. Paul explained here that the pretense of earthly wisdom has no place in the Christian community. Quoting from the prophets, Paul points out that the normal ways of understanding (eye, ear, heart) are unable to decipher God's mysteries.

1 Corinthians 2:10 The Holy Spirit is the reliable source of all human insight into the wisdom of God, for nothing is hidden from the Spirit. None of this insight comes through human wisdom.

Genesis 32:24-31 Jacob's transformation to Israel pertained to the way in which he prevailed. Before he had prevailed over others through trickery; now he prevailed with God, through no human effort. His ambition to win was not changed but oriented in the correct direction. **Peniel.** "The face of God"; Jacob's third great spiritual landmark.

Mark 1:23-26 Normal exorcists would identify themselves by name to some deity or power and then pronounce some authoritative phrase to cast out the demon. Jesus needed no magical formula; He simply told the demon to "be quiet."

Mark 3:10-12 Like the people, the demons recognized something about Jesus. Some scholars believe they knew who He was and gave testimony, while others believe the expression *Son of God* only meant someone who was close to God. Jesus did not want the demons to give testimony to who He was (v. 12).

Mark 3:13-15 Jesus had reached a point in His ministry where He was being persecuted; a few verses earlier, we see a plot against His life was already being hatched. He needed a community as well as followers to take over and spread the message if something happened to Him (as He knew it would).

John 14:16-17 How do people know that they are Christians? How do you and I gain confidence that we are born again by the regenerating power of God's Holy Spirit? The world cannot know because the world cannot accept the Holy Spirit. But Christ told the disciples the Holy Spirit "remains with you and will be in you." The indwelling will be endless: "to be with you forever." No orphans in the family of God, no abandoned people with no place to turn.

Prayer

Name	Request / Praise	Answered

Scripture Notes are excerpted from the *Holman Old Testament Commentary* and *Holman New Testament Commentary* Series. Max Anders, general editor (Nashville: B&H Publishing Group, 1998–2009). Note on "demon posession" is from *Holman Illustrated Bible Dictionary,* s.v. "demonic possession."

Quote is from Lewis Carroll, *Alice's Adventures in Wonderland and Through the Looking Glass* (Edison, NJ: Chartwell Books, 2008), 38.

Memory Verse

"Do not let your hearts be troubled and do not be afraid."
John 14:27, NIV

SMALL GROUP Life

What they experienced

The children learned that the Holy Spirit is their Helper. The Spirit will guide and direct them. They learned that with God on their side, they have the power to overcome evil.

Scene 1: Family Devotion Idea

The children made a wind sock as an illustration of the Holy Spirit. We can't see the Holy Spirit guiding us, just like we can't see the wind moving the wind sock—but He is there. Take this time to share with them an example of when the Holy Spirit moved you to take action.

2nd Take: Family Devotion Idea

Share with your children one of those days when everything that could go wrong did. Talk to them about how we as Christians can use God's power to overcome those situations. We may not be removed from the situation, but with God's help our attitude can be changed!

Family activity

Your children watched several clips from Disney's *The Lion King* over the course of this small group. Have a "Family Movie Night." Fix some popcorn, cuddle up together, and watch the whole movie. Then talk about the movie, relating scenes from the movie to the Christian walk.

SCENE 6

Community

We are made for each other. There is something in every human heart that longs to be known by others and to get to know others in a deeply personal way. Despite our culture's infatuation with rugged individualism and how we are taught to develop a strong sense of independence, most of us list family and friends high among our priorities in life. Yet, having healthy personal relationships and building true community prove remarkably elusive for many. We all know that we need to love and be loved, yet we often find these important connections slipping through our fingers. Our relationships carry with them the potential to bless or to curse. In today's session we'll see how God uses the power of true biblical community to shape us on our journey of transformation.

CONNECT

1 When you were an adolescent, what was the nature of the "gang" of friends with whom you most frequently hung around?

○ Fellow jocks who played and competed with one another

○ The neighborhood pack

○ The nerds

○ A mixed group of people who had similar interests

○ The "alternative" crowd

○ A group of friends who told each other everything

○ A bunch of trouble-makers

○ My youth group at church

○ What gang of friends? I was pretty much a loner.

○ Other

2 Where did your old gang like to go to hang out? What was special about that place?

"Seldom, very seldom, does complete truth belong to any human disclosure; seldom can it happen that something is not a little disguised."

Jane Austen, in Emma

3 What are some of the little disguises that people wear when they're around others? Why do you think we wear disguises at all?

GROW

Leader: Read this paragraph aloud to the group.

The Bible tells us that Solomon was the wisest man who ever lived, his vast knowledge a gift from God. Most scholars believe he penned the Song of Solomon (a love poem) as a young man, the Book of Proverbs in his middle age, and the Book of Ecclesiastes in his later years as he reflected back on life. Seeking to understand how we are formed through relationships, it only makes sense that we should pay attention to Solomon's reflections on the subject.

> 9 **Two are better than one because they have a good reward for their efforts.** 10 **For if either falls, his companion can lift him up; but pity the one who falls without another to lift him up.** 11 **Also, if two lie down together, they can keep warm; but how can one person alone keep warm?** 12 **And if somebody overpowers one person, two can resist him. A cord of three strands is not easily broken.** ECCLESIASTES 4:9-12

Leader/Question #1: Lead your group to explore how we live in the tension between our natural self-centeredness and our need for others.

1. THESE STATEMENTS SEEM A BIT ELEMENTARY TO US. WHY DO YOU THINK SOLOMON BOTHERED TO POINT THEM OUT?

2. SOLOMON GAVE SOME EXAMPLES OF THE BENEFITS OF COMMUNITY THAT WERE RELEVANT TO HIS AUDIENCE. WHAT ARE SOME CONTEMPORARY EXAMPLES YOU CAN GIVE WHICH SHARE THE SAME TRUTH?

Leader/Question #3: Help group members identify people, things, or circumstances that have strengthened them spiritually.

3. HOW DO YOU INTERPRET THE PHRASE "A CORD OF THREE STRANDS IS NOT EASILY BROKEN"? HOW HAS THIS BEEN A PART OF YOUR OWN SPIRITUAL FORMATION?

Jesus had much to say about community and certainly modeled it for us. At times He even challenged people's basic understanding about relationships. Consider the following encounter.

[46] He was still speaking to the crowds when suddenly His mother and brothers were standing outside wanting to speak to Him ... [48] He replied to the one who told Him, "Who is My mother and who are My brothers?" [49] And stretching out His hand toward His disciples, He said, "Here are My mother and My brothers! [50] For whoever does the will of My Father in heaven, that person is My brother and sister and mother." MATTHEW 12:46,48-50

4. WHEN YOU FIRST LOOK AT THIS PASSAGE, WHAT DOES IT SEEM LIKE JESUS IS COMMUNICATING?

5. WHAT ASSUMPTIONS ABOUT RELATIONSHIPS DOES JESUS CHALLENGE HERE?

6. IN WHAT WAYS DO YOU THINK OUR "SPIRITUAL FAMILIES" BECOME LIKE "TRUE FAMILIES" TO US?

Genesis 2:18

Genesis lays the foundation for understanding our great need for relationship, but often key truths are misunderstood or misapplied. "Then the LORD God said, 'It is not good for the man to be alone. I will make a helper who is like him.'" A couple of key truths are embedded in this verse:

- *God affirms that it is "not good" (an anomaly in a world in which things are "very good") for man to be alone; when it comes to relationships, our Creator God knows and provides for our needs even before we are fully aware of them.*
- *The translation "helper" has over the centuries been used as a justification to claim that women are inferior in God's sight to men; in reality, the word in Hebrew is a compound word that means both "to save" and "to be strong."*

As a group, spend some time unpacking Genesis 2:18 and the opportunities and challenges presented in our relationships.

Then God said, "Let Us make man in Our image, according to Our likeness. They will rule the fish of the sea, the birds of the sky, the animals, all the earth, and the creatures that crawl on the earth." GENESIS 1:26

Genesis 1:26 reveals that when the Old Testament speaks of God (Elohim) it is always in the plural—which suggests that God exists in relationship. If God Himself exists in relationship, then our longing for community is one of the ways we bear His image. From the wisdom of Solomon to the ministry of Jesus, we find community a central and defining reality of our spiritual formation.

Leader: Close in prayer or transition to Serve/Go, found on page 101.

SCENE 6

2nd Take

CONNECT
— 10 min.

Leader: Challenge group members to understand why they chose the responses they did, and allow time for interaction.

1. **When you think of your ideal community, what picture comes to mind?**

   ○ A pod of dolphins: effortlessly swimming forward together

   ○ A group of meerkats: only popping your head out when it's your turn for guard duty

   ○ A team of mountain-climbers: hooked together ... just in case

   ○ An athletic team: love those pep rallies!

   ○ _____ (your choice)

2. **Name a movie, story, or novel you've watched or read which expresses your ideal community in a compelling way. What made it so appealing?**

GROW

40–50 min.

Through the selfless example of Jesus and His life in community with His disciples, the value of authentic redemptive relationships became a defining feature of their everyday lives. The disciples and then the early church would continue to discover the power of this theme that God had woven into the hearts of man as they learned to live out genuine care and concern for each other.

> ¹⁴ **Then Jesus returned to Galilee in the power of the Spirit, and news about Him spread throughout the entire vicinity. ¹⁵ He was teaching in their synagogues, being acclaimed by everyone.**
> ¹⁶ **He came to Nazareth, where He had been brought up. As usual, He entered the synagogue on the Sabbath day and stood up to read. ¹⁷ The scroll of the prophet Isaiah was given to Him, and unrolling the scroll, He found the place where it was written:**
> > ¹⁸ **"The Spirit of the Lord is on Me,**
> > **because He has anointed Me**
> > **to preach good news to the poor.**
> > **He has sent Me**
> > **to proclaim freedom to the captives**
> > **and recovery of sight to the blind,**
> > **to set free the oppressed,**
> > ¹⁹ **to proclaim the year of the Lord's favor."**
>
> LUKE 4:14-19

Leader/ Question #1: Ask the group to share stories they remember from the Gospels of the ways that Jesus "preached good news," "proclaimed freedom for captives," and "set free the oppressed."

1. OF ALL THE SCRIPTURES JESUS COULD HAVE CHOSEN, WHY DO YOU THINK HE READ FROM THIS OLD TESTAMENT PROPHECY? SHARE WAYS THAT THESE WORDS APPROPRIATELY DESCRIBE THE MINISTRY OF JESUS.

2. HOW DO YOU THINK OUR COMMUNITIES TODAY CAN LIVE OUT THE HEART OF JESUS' EARTHLY REDEMPTIVE MISSION?

[24] **Let us be concerned about one another in order to promote love and good works,** [25] **not staying away from our meetings, as some habitually do, but encouraging each other, and all the more as you see the day drawing near.** HEBREWS 10:24-25

3. HOW DO YOU THINK SHOWING CONCERN FOR EACH OTHER MIGHT PROMOTE LOVE AND GOOD WORKS?

Leader/ Question #4: Accountability works best in community.

4. THE TERM WE OFTEN USE FOR GENUINE "CONCERN" AIMED AT "PROMOTING LOVE AND GOOD WORKS" IS ACCOUNTABILITY. DO YOU HAVE A SYSTEM OF ACCOUNTABILITY BUILT INTO YOUR LIFE RIGHT NOW? WHY OR WHY NOT?

Leader/ Question #5: Just as every person matters to God, so every person matters to a community of believers (see Ephesians 4:1-4).

5. THE BIBLE DOESN'T NORMALLY SEEM TO BE CONCERNED WITH KEEPING "ATTENDANCE RECORDS." WHY DO YOU THINK THIS PASSAGE MENTIONS THE IMPORTANCE OF NOT MISSING MEETING TOGETHER?

[1] I want you to get out there and walk—better yet, run!—on the road God called you to travel. I don't want any of you sitting around on your hands. I don't want anyone strolling off, down some path that goes nowhere. [2] And mark that you do this with humility and discipline—not in fits and starts, but steadily, pouring yourselves out for each other in acts of love, [3] alert at noticing differences and quick at mending fences.

[4] You were all called to travel on the same road and in the same direction, so stay together, both outwardly and inwardly.
EPHESIANS 4:1-4, THE MESSAGE

6. THERE IS A SENSE OF URGENCY TO HEBREWS 10:24-25 AND EPHESIANS 4:1-4. WHY MIGHT WE
   NEED COMMUNITY "ALL THE MORE" WHEN TIMES ARE DIFFICULT?

7. WHAT DOES IT MEAN TO "STAY TOGETHER, BOTH OUTWARDLY AND INWARDLY"?

Redemptive communities embody the heart of Jesus' mission: to bring freedom to the captives, sight
to the blind, and to trade the ashes of brokenness for the beauty of restoration. While we are not
all identical, the true mark of biblical community is this: the one thing we have in common (Jesus
Christ) is more important than all of our differences. And the work of redemptive community then
flows from our unified hearts as we use our differences to reach out to others with the hope that we
have in Christ.

SERVE ☞ GO

10 min.

While we know that Christian community is important for believers, we can also easily see the potential that our small groups have for impacting the broader community.

> **Many Christ-followers spend a good deal of time talking about community, but many of us don't even know our own neighbors. As a group, set out this week with the goal to meet or get to know at least one neighbor in a more personal way. Here are some suggestions:**
>
> › In biblical times, sharing a meal was an important sign of acceptance. Invite a neighbor over for a "family style" dinner this week.
>
> › Look around for projects that you can help a neighbor with. Offering to mow a lawn while someone is on vacation or helping them clean out a garage can break down barriers.
>
> › Women tend to communicate best face-to-face and men side-by-side. If you're female, invite another lady over for brunch or coffee. If you're a guy, invite a neighbor over to watch the game with you instead of watching it by yourself. If you're a parent, set a play date with the kids; you'd be surprised how much meaningful conversation you can have when the kids are playing with new friends.
>
> **Come prepared to share with the group next week on what you discovered during your "ministry of presence" assignment.**

Leader: Close by standing, sitting, or kneeling in a circle as a group. Have everyone pray for the person on their left; as the leader, close by thanking God for the gift and power of redemptive community.

Scripture Notes

Ecclesiastes 4:9-12 Scripture warns us about those who separate themselves from others. This can make us more vulnerable to spiritual attack (1 Peter 5:8-9). We can all be deceived, so we need others to keep us accountable (Hebrews 3:13). The effect of two people working in harmony together can be much greater than those two laboring on their own. Times of pain and struggle come upon all of us, and it is truly tragic when there is no support.

Matthew 12:46,48-50 Jesus loved and took care of His earthly family and meant them no insult. He simply needed to make a point about a more significant family. Christ uses the illustration of family to expand on His declaration that having Israelite blood was not enough to enter the kingdom (vv. 39-45). This new family was fathered by God and determined by a relationship with the Heavenly Father.

Luke 4:14-19 While Satan tried to lead Jesus to Jerusalem to perform miracles before the multitudes, the Spirit guided Christ to rural Galilee, to teach in small places of worship. He escaped the major political center and taught fishermen, farmers, and traders. People in Galilee thronged to Him. But then it was time for Him to go home to Nazareth. There, He was given the honor of reading from the scroll and preaching during the synagogue service.

Hebrews 10:24-25 **promote love and good works.** As Christians, we have a corporate responsibility to help others who stumble and falter. **staying away from our meetings.** Christians who meet together with the aim of promoting godliness and love for one another can be remarkably successful in their ventures. Regular fellowship is an essential ingredient in Christian growth. Persecution may have led to some of the Hebrew Christians dropping out of the fellowship. The remedy they needed was to start meeting again. The following verses (vv. 26-31) show the result of neglecting to meet with other believers.

Prayer

Name	Request / Praise	Answered

Scripture Notes are excerpted from the *Holman Old Testament Commentary* and *Holman New Testament Commentary* Series. Max Anders, general editor (Nashville: B&H Publishing Group, 1998–2009).

Quote is from Jane Austen, *Emma* (New York: Random House, 2001), 314.

Memory Verse

"A friend loves at all times."
Proverbs 17:17, NIV

SMALL GROUP *Life* (er)

What they experienced

The children learned about who is in their community and the importance of choosing friends with good character. They also learned the importance of being a good friend.

Scene 1: Family Devotion Idea

The children made a "good" character fruit tree and an "evil" character fruit tree. They then listed friends with "good fruit." Ask your children about their friends. Help them discern when a friend is not bearing good fruit.

2nd Take: Family Devotion Idea

Ask your children if they have gone out of their way to be kind to a friend. Ask them if a friend has gone out of their way to help them. Talk about the importance of being a good friend. Having good friendships will influence their spiritual lives.

Family activity

Think of a family friend that you and your children can help this week. Could you run errands, fix dinner, wash their car, do yard work? You will get a blessing when you do!

LEADER'S GUIDE
General Tips

Tips on facilitating a great small-group experience are on pages 108–111.

"Out of the Smaller Group Bucket" studies for the children can be downloaded at *www.lifeway.com/smallgrouplife.* Each lesson will have its own list of items you need to supply the children's teacher or parent volunteer.

Small(er) Group Life is found at the end of each Scene and helps families engage their children in the week's conversation. A memory verse is highlighted as well as devotion ideas and a family activity.

Video downloads are available to complement each week's meeting at *www.lifeway.com/sgl.* These can be e-mailed to members beforehand, or you may choose to interact with the video during each meeting.

CONNECT: Each Connect section has questions with which your group can interact. A quote is also provided on the fourth page of each Scene. You can choose to e-mail the quote to members before your session, or you might decide to discuss it during your meeting.

Connect questions serve as a weekly icebreaker allowing members to get to know one another better and to connect with their own hearts at a deeper level. There are no right or wrong answers.

GROW: A brief description of the theme for each week's meeting is detailed later in the Leader's Guide.

SERVE/GO: Serve/Go provides suggested missional opportunities for your group each Scene. You will want to decide together how often to participate and what level of accountability to bring. Allowing time at the beginning of each meeting or during the Serve/Go time to celebrate "success" stories will serve as continued motivation for group members to participate!

NOTES: _____

_____

Scene 1: Purpose

Many Christians are not aware of the ways they've been formed and for what purposes their spiritual formation can serve. Not only does God redeem our personal stories, but He asks us to trust Him as He works through our stories in the lives of others. Using Gideon as an example of someone who doubted his own abilities and purpose, someone who has bought into the "my mess is too much for God" lie, this experience will help group members begin to see that they have been created for and are being transformed into more than what they've become.

CONNECT: Encourage each member to participate from the beginning. This will establish a pattern of participation that enriches the community.

GROW: The story of Gideon is found in Judges 6–7, so you might want to read those two chapters to better understand the context for the verses that will be used throughout this Purpose experience. The people of God had been living in disobedience to Him for some time when the story begins, resulting in seven years of oppression by the Midianites. There are many interesting subplots to the Gideon story, but you'll want to stay focused on the given passages, which are transformational in nature. Verses from Jeremiah are used in the Second Take to push further into members' own stories.

SERVE/GO: Be sure to follow up with those who are helped, looking for opportunities to further develop relationships.

NOTES:

Scene 2: Enemy

Because evil in the world can be disorienting, we often mistake lies for the truth, failing to identify the real enemy—the Villain—in our stories. This lesson is important because it will help group members identify the Villain, his origins, and how this contributes to our spiritual deformation.

PREPARATION: You will need to obtain a copy of the DVD *Gladiator* (Dreamworks, 1999) for Second Take.

CONNECT: Encourage each member to participate from the beginning. This will establish a pattern of participation that enriches the community.

GROW: Because we are given teaching about our enemy the Devil in small portions throughout the Bible, this study may seem to hop around a bit. At times he is disguised as a beast: in Genesis a serpent and in Revelation a dragon. Other times he is described metaphorically or by the evil actions for which he is known. Make no mistake though, the Enemy is very real. Some group members may be so familiar with Satan as a caricature that they have come to dismiss him as a threat. Once we see the Enemy for who he is and what he can do, we are able to combat him effectively using wisdom from Scripture.

SERVE/GO: Encourage group members to go ahead and write down names of neighbors or people they could contact.

NOTES:

Scene 3: Redemption

Even as we are spiritually formed, we still make some poor decisions, experience failure, and both break hearts and have our hearts broken. But Jesus' mission as He describes it in Luke 4 promises to buy it all back. Knowing how redemption is alive in group members' formation gives greater clarity and a capacity to live the sort of life God had in mind when He created us.

PREPARATION: You will need to obtain a copy of the DVD *Heart and Souls* (Universal Studios, 1998) for Second Take's Connect.

CONNECT: Encourage participation. Try not to let one person dominate the conversation.

GROW: Redemption is a key theme in Scripture, and this study tries to go beyond the basic theological concept to explore some of the things that we have been redeemed from and are being redeemed from. Seeing Jesus as our Hero-Redeemer in the ongoing spiritual battles that we face, not just for our salvation, is important to our spiritual formation. You may have to work hard to move beyond the Roman Road approach to these verses, which many group members will know.

SERVE/GO: Be prepared with some information about the prison ministries listed on page 53, if possible, for group members who may be interested.

NOTES:

Scene 4: Atonement

As we do life together, we cannot help but make mistakes along our formative journeys. While emotional and mental paralysis and passivity contribute to a reclusive "hunker-down" mentality, Christ's atonement opens the door to deep change, a constitutional makeover. This transformation empowers us to move on, continuing our spiritual pilgrimage into greater Christlikeness.

PREPARATION: You will need to obtain a copy of the movie *Stranger than Fiction* (Columbia Pictures, 2006) for the first week's Connect. You may need a guitar, MP3 player, or worship DVD for Connect in Second Take. You may need the song or lyrics for "Jesus Paid It All" in Serve/Go.

CONNECT: See music recommendation on page 64, Second Take, for the Connect activity. If your group has someone who is gifted to lead in worship, have him or her help find a song with an atonement theme.

GROW: The act of atonement was designed to demonstrate two important things. First, God treated the sin of His people seriously. But second, God loved His people and graciously provided the means to restore their relationship with Him. The challenge again in this study will be to move beyond a discussion of atonement as a theological concept and instead focus upon what it means for your journey with God.

SERVE/GO: Depending on the group makeup, you could consider this option as an individual or family ministry.

NOTES:

Scene 5: Mystery

We tend to default to the common life we see everyday—our routes to and from work, the people in our various communities, and daily routines. We have a tendency to be drawn into our own stories and battles while unaware of a Larger Story (see p. 29) behind the spiritual veil—the veil that separates the physical world from the spiritual one—where there is a very real battle being fought for our hearts.

PREPARATION: You can bring some music to play during the Connect activity for Second Take. Members also need their Bibles, pens, journals, and/or paper for this Connect, so be sure to remind them at the end of week one.

Gather information about your church's missions opportunities to share with the group during Serve/Go.

CONNECT: Instrumental music may help members to relax during the meditation exercise in Second Take.

GROW: Since this study is about mystery, it's important that you as a leader feel comfortable with mystery and paradox. Often we feel pressured to have all the answers or to stay within our systems of thought. We are reminded here that God is comfortable with mystery. Jesus demonstrated throughout His ministry on earth that He was comfortable with mystery. We want to lead members to embrace mystery as well.

SERVE/GO: You might consider having members who have been on mission trips before share during Serve/Go.

NOTES:

Scene 6: Community

This lesson is about the ways that community figures into your spiritual formation. God exists in community eternally. God created community in the original family and said that it was good. Jesus chose community as the vehicle for His mission. Community continues to be the best context in which Jesus' mission of healing and restoration takes place.

CONNECT: Encourage each member to participate from the beginning. This will establish a pattern of participation that enriches the community.

GROW: One of the most significant barriers to experiencing redemptive community is our natural inclination to hide our true selves. Hopefully, you are beginning to see people willing to share and striving for authentic relationships. The Bible verses used in this study reinforce the point that God created us for community. We are better together, and together as a small group we can have a great Kingdom impact upon our broader communities.

SERVE/GO: Depending on the group makeup, you could consider this option as an individual or family ministry.

NOTES:

WELCOME TO COMMUNITY!

Meeting together to study God's Word and experience life together is an exciting adventure. A small group is ... *a group of people unwilling to settle for anything less than redemptive community.*

Core Values

COMMUNITY: God is relational, so He created us to live in relationship with Him and each other. Authentic community involves sharing life together and connecting on many levels with others in our group.

GROUP PROCESS: Developing authentic community takes time. It's a journey of sharing our stories with each other and learning together. Every healthy group goes through stages over a period of months or years. We begin with the birth of a new group, then deepen our relationships in the growth and development stages.

INTERACTIVE BIBLE STUDY: God gave the Bible as our instruction manual for life. We need to deepen our understanding of God's Word. People learn and remember more as they wrestle with truth and learn from others. Bible discovery and group interaction enhance growth.

EXPERIENTIAL GROWTH: Beyond solely reading, studying, and dissecting the Bible, being a disciple of Christ involves reunifying knowledge with experience. We do this by taking questions to God, opening a dialogue with our hearts (instead of killing desire), and utilizing other ways to listen to God speak (other people, nature, art, movies, circumstances). Experiential growth is always grounded in the Bible as God's primary revelation and our ultimate truth-source.

POWER OF GOD: Processes and strategies will be ineffective unless we invite and embrace the presence and power of God. In order to experience community and growth, Jesus needs to be the centerpiece of our group experiences and the Holy Spirit must be at work.

REDEMPTIVE COMMUNITY: Healing best occurs within the context of community and relationships. It's vital to see ourselves through the eyes of others, share our stories, and ultimately find freedom from the secrets and lies that enslave our souls.

MISSION: God has invited us into a larger story with a great mission of setting captives free and healing the broken-hearted (Isaiah 61:1-2). However, we can only join in this mission to the degree that we've let Jesus bind up our wounds and set us free. Others will be attracted to an authentic redemptive community.

SHARING YOUR STORIES

The sessions of Small Group Life are designed to help you share a bit of your personal lives with the other people in your group as you experience life together. Through your time together, each member of the group is encouraged to move from low risk, less personal sharing to higher risk communication. Real community will not develop apart from increasing intimacy over time.

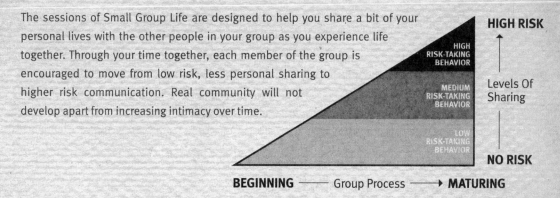

SHARING YOUR LIVES

As you share your lives together during this time, it's important to recognize that it's God who brought each person to this group, gifting the individuals to play a vital role in the group (1 Corinthians 12:1). Each of you was uniquely designed to contribute in your own unique way to building into the lives of the other people in your group. As you get to know one another better, consider the following four areas that will be unique for each person. These areas will help you get a "grip" on how you can better support others and how they can support you.

G – SPIRITUAL GIFTS:
God has given you unique spiritual gifts (1 Corinthians 12; Romans 12:3-8; Ephesians 4:1-16).

R – RESOURCES:
You have resources that perhaps only you can share, including skill, abilities, possessions, money, and time (Acts 2:44-47; Ecclesiastes 4:9-12).

I – INDIVIDUAL EXPERIENCES:
You have past experiences, both good and bad, that God can use to strengthen and encourage others (2 Corinthians 1:3-7; Romans 8:28).

P – PASSIONS:
There are things that excite and motivate you. God has given you those desires and passions to use for His purposes (Psalm 37:4,23; Proverbs 3:5-6,13-18).

To better understand how a group should function and develop in these four areas, consider taking your group on a journey in community using the Serendipity study entitled *Great Beginnings*.

LEADING A SMALL GROUP

You will find a great deal of helpful information in this section that will be crucial for success as you lead your group.

Reading through this section and utilizing the suggested principles and practices will greatly enhance the group experience. First is to accept the limitations of leadership. You cannot transform a life. You must lead your group to the Bible, the Holy Spirit, and the power of Christian community. By doing so your group will have all the tools necessary to draw closer to God and to each other, and to experience heart transformation.

MAKE THE FOLLOWING THINGS AVAILABLE AT EACH SESSION:

+ *Small Group Life* book for each attendee
+ A Bible for each attendee
+ Snacks and refreshments (encourage everyone to bring something unprepared)
+ Pens or pencils for each participant

The Setting and General Tips

#1 Prepare for each meeting by reviewing the material, praying for each group member, asking the Holy Spirit to join you, and making Jesus the centerpiece of every experience.

#2 Create the right environment by making sure chairs are arranged so each person can see every other attendee. Set the room temperature at 69 degrees. If meeting in a home, make sure pets are where they cannot interrupt the meeting. Request that cell phones be turned off unless someone is expecting an emergency call. Have music playing as people arrive (volume low enough for people to converse) and, if possible, burn a sweet-smelling candle.

#3 Try to have soft drinks and coffee available for early arrivals.

#4 Have someone with the spiritual gift of hospitality ready to make any new attendees feel welcome.

#5 Be sure there is adequate lighting so that everyone can read without straining.

#6 Think of ways to connect with group members away from group time. The amount of participation you have during your group meetings is directly related to the amount of time you connect with your group members away from the group meeting.

#7 There are four types of questions used in each session: Observation (What is the passage telling us?), Interpretation (What does the passage mean?), Self-revelation (How am I doing in light of the truth unveiled?), and Application (Now that I know what I know, what will I do to integrate this truth into my life?). You won't be able to use all the questions in each study, but be sure to use some from each.

#8 Don't lose patience about the depth of relationship group members are experiencing. Building real Christian community takes time.

#9 Be sure pens or pencils are available for attendees at each meeting.

#10 Never ask someone to pray aloud without first asking their permission.

Leading Meetings

#1 Before the Connect sections, do not say, "Now we're going to do an icebreaker." The entire session should feel like a conversation from beginning to end, not a classroom experience.

#2 Be certain every member responds to the icebreaker questions. The goal is for every person to hear his or her own voice early in the meeting. People will then feel comfortable to converse later on. If members can't think of a response, let them know you'll come back to them after the others have spoken.

#3 Remember, a great group leader talks less than 10 percent of the time. If you ask a question and no one answers, just wait. If you create an environment where you fill the gaps of silence, the group will quickly learn they don't need to join you in the conversation.

#4 Don't be hesitant to call people by name as you ask them to respond to questions or to give their opinions. Be sensitive, but engage everyone in the conversation.

#5 Don't ask people to read aloud unless you have gotten their permission prior to the meeting. Feel free to ask for volunteers to read.

#6 Watch your time. If discussion extends past the time limits suggested, offer the option of pressing on into other discussions or continuing the current content into your next meeting.

REMEMBER: People and their needs are always more important than completing your agenda or finishing all the questions.

#7 Use sub-grouping if there are more than eight people in the group, particularly during Grow.

GROUP DIRECTORY

Write your name on this page. Pass your books around and ask your group members to fill in their names and contact information in each other's books.

YOUR NAME: _____

NAME: _____   **NAME:** _____

ADDRESS: _____   ADDRESS: _____

CITY: _____ ZIP CODE: _____   CITY: _____ ZIP CODE: _____

HOME PHONE: _____   HOME PHONE: _____

MOBILE PHONE: _____   MOBILE PHONE: _____

E-MAIL: _____   E-MAIL: _____

NAME: _____   **NAME:** _____

ADDRESS: _____   ADDRESS: _____

CITY: _____ ZIP CODE: _____   CITY: _____ ZIP CODE: _____

HOME PHONE: _____   HOME PHONE: _____

MOBILE PHONE: _____   MOBILE PHONE: _____

E-MAIL: _____   E-MAIL: _____

NAME: _____   **NAME:** _____

ADDRESS: _____   ADDRESS: _____

CITY: _____ ZIP CODE: _____   CITY: _____ ZIP CODE: _____

HOME PHONE: _____   HOME PHONE: _____

MOBILE PHONE: _____   MOBILE PHONE: _____

E-MAIL: _____   E-MAIL: _____

NAME: _____   **NAME:** _____

ADDRESS: _____   ADDRESS: _____

CITY: _____ ZIP CODE: _____   CITY: _____ ZIP CODE: _____

HOME PHONE: _____   HOME PHONE: _____

MOBILE PHONE: _____   MOBILE PHONE: _____

E-MAIL: _____   E-MAIL: _____

NAME: _____   **NAME:** _____

ADDRESS: _____   ADDRESS: _____

CITY: _____ ZIP CODE: _____   CITY: _____ ZIP CODE: _____

HOME PHONE: _____   HOME PHONE: _____

MOBILE PHONE: _____   MOBILE PHONE: _____

E-MAIL: _____   E-MAIL: _____

NAME: _____   **NAME:** _____

ADDRESS: _____   ADDRESS: _____

CITY: _____ ZIP CODE: _____   CITY: _____ ZIP CODE: _____

HOME PHONE: _____   HOME PHONE: _____

MOBILE PHONE: _____   MOBILE PHONE: _____

E-MAIL: _____   E-MAIL: _____